MY LIFE
WITH A
Dandelion

SHEA M. JACKSON

Order this book online at www.trafford.com
or email orders@trafford.com

Most Trafford titles are also available at major online book retailers.

Printed in the United States of America.

ISBN: 978-1-4669-7738-9 (sc)
ISBN: 978-1-4669-7737-2 (e)

Trafford rev. 03/19/2013

Trafford
PUBLISHING   www.trafford.com

North America & international
toll-free: 1 888 232 4444 (USA & Canada)
phone: 250 383 6864 ♦ fax: 812 355 4082

TABLE OF CONTENTS

DEDICATION

To my husband, Robby Jackson, Jr., who walked this journey by my side and never allowed me to stop moving forward or question his love for me.

To my sons, Tate and Corey, who traveled through the wilderness with us and were the shining light of God for many of those days.

To my daughter, "LuLu", who I have had the honor to know and learn from.

Most of all, to my Heavenly Father, who I give all the glory and honor to for who I have become through this journey. I know that I'm still a work in progress and may all I say and do always honor and glorify Him.

Thank you to our WellSpring Community Church family who welcomed us with open arms years ago and who continues to love and encourage us. We are blessed to be traveling on this life's journey with you.

Thank you to our Millbrook Community Theatre family who has given us the opportunity to use our gifts and talents to shine for His glory. You have been instrumental in LuLu's social growth and the love and kindness that you've shown our family is precious.

I would like to thank Karla A. McGhee for her many hours of editing my manuscript and crossing out all of my quotation marks. Thank you for your honesty and wisdom. You have been priceless in helping me make this book a reality. Welcome to the South my friend! Yes, Ma'am!

Thank you to Ms. Bonnie U. Holland who encouraged me to share this amazing story in book form. You and Mr. Gene will always have a special place in our hearts.

Thank you to all those friends and family who are too numerous to name who have encouraged us along the way. May you know that we are so very grateful that you are in our lives!

PURPOSE

By reading about my journey of the heart—trials, tribulations and overall triumphs, I hope that you are encouraged by the miracles that my family and I have witnessed in the life of my special needs daughter. When things looked the darkest, it was our heavenly Father that gave us the light to continue to move forward in our "wilderness" journey.

While most of these pages have come directly from the pages of my personal journal, I have chosen to omit the names of some people and places to protect both the innocent and guilty. I've also chosen to refer to my daughter in this story by her nickname, "LuLu", as that is what she likes to be called. I will honestly admit to you that this book has brought healing to me, although it was difficult and very painful for me to relive some of the events of the past. My hope for you, dear reader, is that you will acquire a better understanding of just how precious life truly is and that no life should be considered less valuable than another.

My husband and I have had the privilege of living in the house that belonged to his grandmother. We've been able to raise our three children in the same house that holds so many childhood memories for him. It's located in Millbrook, Alabama—north of the State's Capitol, Montgomery. Living in this city has given us the warm feeling of family and a sense of comfort with its southern charm and friendly faces. With our corner lot, our azalea filled yard and our house full of memories, I sat down to record every step of my journey with our little "dandelion".

"Why, yet you do not know what tomorrow will bring.
What is your life?
For you are a mist that appears for a little time and then vanishes."
James 4:14

Chapter 1

A Dandelion—
An Unwanted Weed or Beloved
"Blow-it Flower"? . . .

The dandelion has been despised by gardeners and home owners for years because they seem to grow everywhere and are very resilient. Many people cringe when they see the yellow heads of this weed waving in the springtime breeze on their carefully manicured lawns. Many Saturday mornings in the south, you can see serious homeowners out in their yards and gardens with a variety of tools and chemicals trying to get rid of these cheerful weeds in hopes of having a perfect lawn and saving their flowerbeds from being overtaken by this willful weed. The poor dandelion gets an unfair assessment in my opinion. This wonderful weed is an important food source to many animals and it's also useful to humans as it can be used for food and medicine. No part of the dandelion weed is useless—from the root all the way up to the top of the flower. Just like the dandelion, the world viewed my daughter as a useless, unwanted weed, but I had my own view of her and, like the dandelion, it was anything but useless.

We live in a society today that places a greater value on people who can successfully contribute to its fast paced needs. People are highly valued if they hold prestigious, powerful jobs, make more money than they need or have a wall of awards or degrees. People are highly valued if they have no special limitations to hold them or others from being a productive citizen. But, anyone who falls outside the lines of what our society defines as "normal" is often looked upon, not as a blessing, but a burden. Just because our society places a greater value on people without special needs doesn't mean that

1

God has the same perspective. When God creates a person, He creates that person to accomplish *HIS* divine purposes. Please keep in mind that God's purposes may not be the same as our purposes. *All* life is precious to God.

I have always wanted to be a mother for as long as I can remember. Many hours were spent writing out the names of my future children and dreaming of what life would be like as their mother. I hoped for several children as I am an only child and was often very lonely. During those lonely times I made a lot of use of my extraordinary imagination by daydreaming of my future. Even as a young child I was definitely a planner. But what I didn't plan on was having a child with special needs. Nothing could have prepared me for the journey—not even a hundred years of detailed planning.

There are many times in our lives that we plan for things like vacations, weddings and children and the heavenly Father allows changes in our plans to help us become who He created us to be. As a planner, I like to use calendars that allow you to see the whole month at once—no little daily calendar will do for me. I will make lists in my sleep of events and items to be added to our family calendar. I guess that most of this "planning ahead" comes from the fact that as a child, I could not control a lot of what happened to me. Overcoming all the obstacles of my childhood prepared me for life with my special needs daughter.

Having a child with special needs can make you feel isolated, overwhelmed and exhausted. I read somewhere that being a parent of a special needs child is like planning for a special vacation to somewhere tropical. You have packed lightly for the warm climate and have planned to visit all the breath-taking sights. It is only when the plane lands that you realize that you are not in a tropical place— very far from it. You are in the middle of a snowstorm! You begin to think about how this could have happened. You quickly search for your tickets to explain that this is not your destination. Your thoughts are brought to your lightweight clothing. You don't even have a coat!

How are you going to survive this trip? You feel as if you are in the twilight zone as you flag down the flight attendant and try to explain your problem. You are met with her bright smile, but she is acting like she isn't hearing a word that you are saying. As you are escorted down the aisle toward the exit, you continue to try to explain your dilemma. As you mix in with the other passengers, you quickly realize that you are not prepared for what is happening. You try to talk to everyone that you see, and all of them think that you are crazy and avoid you. You feel that you are all alone and no matter who you talk to, no one can understand your distress. You have to make a choice: Make the best out of this trip or continue to sit and complain.

I had to make a choice when I realized that my daughter was developmentally and mentally delayed. I had planned to welcome a healthy baby girl and our days together were supposed to be precious and delightful—after all, that is what I had been planning for years. But when the time came to share our days together, it was not exactly that way at all—it was nothing like I had planned. I had to make a choice. I could make the best out of it or dwell on the fact that she was "special". I made the choice to make the best of it—after all she was a gift from God and I wasn't about to be ungrateful. If I had dwelt on the fact that she was "special", then I would have missed out on the miracles and the wisdom that this experience taught me. I would have missed out on the beautiful young woman that she is today.

LuLu had a language all her own and sometimes it was difficult to decipher. Although there were times that her language made perfect sense. She called brooms "a sweep-it" (makes sense) and a car was called "a drive-it". (that makes sense as well) We began to quickly understand that even though she may not know the correct name for an object, she did get their purpose. Hence the name "blow-it flower" for her beloved dandelions that she could not wait to get her hands on each time she spotted one. Watching her skip from one "blow-it flower" to another brought my heart great joy and renewed my strength in hope that she would be able to lead a productive life despite what we were told by the doctors. Her care-free attitude and joy in the little things made me realize that I had so very much to be grateful for. The picture on the front cover of this book was taken at the time of my great revelation—the picture captures not only my daughter's love for life but a mark in a time in my life when I truly began to cherish the little things and be grateful for every blessing—taking nothing for granted. Seeing her pick a "blow-it flower" and blow the white fluff into the air, was priceless! Watching her amazement as the little white parachute tufts carried the seeds high above our heads and to destinations unknown to us was a great joy. The care-free innocence of childhood is often lost so quickly in this world. It's a pity that too many parents wish these precious moments away so that their children can be more independent and require less supervision. I decided that day that no matter what came our way, with the help of my Heavenly Father, I was going to be victorious. I was going to overcome all the obstacles that lay ahead in our journey and that I didn't want to have any regrets. I asked the Father for His guidance and stood firm on His promise to never leave me. My wilderness journey was just beginning and I thought that I was well prepared—I was wrong. I know now why we should walk by faith and not by sight because if I had known what was on the road ahead, I would have surely let fear win.

I have to admit that this wilderness journey was not at all easy! What part of a wilderness journey ever is? The whole purpose for the "wilderness experience" is to strengthen us—emotionally, physically and spiritually. Being in the middle of a desert-like place prepares us to be "thirsty" for help and to depend on God alone. This is just what happened to me. When I saw my daughter with her "blow-it flower" that day, I knew that she was not useless. I began to see that she had a purpose that was way beyond what I could have ever imagined. I began to see her as a beautiful "blow-it flower" and not as the unwanted weed that the world saw.

"We walk by faith, not by sight." 2 Corinthians 5:7

"For we are God's workmanship,
created in Christ Jesus to do good works,
which God prepared in advance for us to do."

Ephesians 2:10

Chapter 2

PLAN FOR THE CHANGES

(THEY OFTEN PREPARE US FOR PURPOSE)

There are many things in life that happens to us that are beyond our control. I have learned that as much as I plan, my plans most likely will change. I have been blessed with the ability to quickly come up with a "plan B" should the original plan change. (which happens more often than not.) I often laugh and wonder why I even bother with planning anything, but I always try to be prepared for everything—even the changes.

As creatures of habit, we like things to stay the same. We enjoy sitting in the same place each Sunday at church, parking in the same parking space at work and having the same daily routines that make us comfortable. We have accepted the changes of the seasons, even though I, having lived in the South all my life, often complain about the humid summers that wreak havoc on my fine hair and quickly welcome the drier, cool air of fall. Although the change to winter makes me even more thankful for the heat of summer days. It's when we are out of our comfort zones that make us truly grateful for changes—even though we may not realize it at the time.

I guess if I'm going to tell you about the great miracles that I witnessed in my daughter's life, I need to give you some background—a reference point so that you can see just where we came from and how far we have traveled. I will begin with a little background on myself and allow you to see just how God molded me for the important mission of being the mother of *LuLu*. These memories are both precious and bittersweet—intertwined into the very fabric of mind. My mother use to tell me that we are given bad times to test us and help us to be strong and thankful for the good times. I agree. The following is a background of life before *LuLu* and our life after her arrival. Much of the material in this chapter makes me sad, but I thought that you need to know it to be able to better understand the battle that we fought for many years.

My life has always been full of many changes, just as any other person. I was born to two young parents who divorced before I was two years old. I do not have any siblings and many of my days as a child were very lonely.

My mother struggled as a single parent—moving from one place to another seeking a safe neighborhood that she could afford. There were very few—even at that time. I was in and out of several schools before I was even ten years old. I had to make myself adjust to all of the changes and I began to look forward to the next "adventure" with some sort of cheerful anticipation. I *planned* to be a cheerful and obedient daughter. I knew that my mother didn't need to stress about anything else. I made friends quite easily and I was drawn to those children who were shy and that separated themselves from the rest of the class. I was often called upon by teachers to assist these withdrawn children with many of the daily tasks of school and I looked forward to the new things that these special souls would learn and accomplish each day. I could often be found on the playground surrounded by a gaggle of little girls and boys anticipating another fairytale with a twist. I remember that their favorite story was *Goldilocks and the Three Bears*. In my version, Goldilocks was a disobedient young girl that didn't listen to her mother about the dangers of the woods. She made some pretty poor choices and had to deal with the consequences of those choices and learn to make better choices in the future. I remember having a funny voice and over-the-top action for each character. I'm sure that the view from outside our circle was quite comical! This was the beginning of my revelation that I was going to be used for a greater purpose—even if I didn't truly understand it.

Before I was ten years old, my mother met Marshall, a man that was kind and loving to us both. I couldn't have been happier! My life was pretty good during this time. I was finally able to stay in the same school for two years in a row and I was thrilled at the announcement of wedding plans at the conclusion of my mother's schooling for her RN degree. That day never came! Three months before she was to graduate from nursing school, she was in a terrible, single automobile accident and died. She was a very young woman of just over thirty years old and I was a less than a month away from being twelve—Christmas was only days away and my life was about to change again!

Since my mother and Marshall were not yet married, I was sent to live with my mother's family—almost two-hundred miles away. There were so many changes coming at me that I was overwhelmed for a very long time. My daily life in the hustle and bustle of a busy city life was exchanged for a slower paced one. I was surrounded by my family consisting of my grandmother, aunts, uncles and cousins, but I felt so very lonely. Marshall was encouraged to move on with his life and we lost contact for many years. I withdrew for a while and I found comfort in some of the things that were left behind by my mother . . . . like her clothes—I could sit and smell them for hours as they still carried the scent of her perfume on them. I missed the school friends that I had made and I wondered if I would be chosen to assist with the "quiet" classmates at the new school.

Even though I had so many unanswered questions, but at the same time, I felt a great sense of peace. I knew that the Father was with me and I kept hearing the words, "have faith—just have faith" in my heart. I did, indeed have faith, even if it was the size of a mustard seed. But that's all that He needs—just a little faith. That small amount of faith that I had grew into an amazing confidence in Him. I promised to trust Him with everything—even the smallest things. I knew that He would never leave me and that He would give me the strength to do what needed to be done. (My life verse:

Philippians 4:13) I was beginning to understand that my life was going to be anything but ordinary and boring.

Fast forward to the beginning of my adult life, I married Robby, who I had dated my whole junior and senior years of high school. We were married only three months after my high school graduation and many people felt that our marriage wouldn't work because Robby was a divorced father that was raising a young son from the previous marriage. His son, Tate was only two years old when we married and I could not have been happier with this little guy if I'd given birth to him myself! His sweet smile and large, brown eyes made my heart melt. Many of my high school friends asked me how I could settle down and be a wife and mom at such an early age. I told them that I knew that I was born for this role and that my love for Robby and for children outweighed anything else and I wished them luck where ever their separate roads were taking them. I do not have any regrets about these choices—Robby is my best friend and our love is stronger than ever before and we continue to journey together down life's road . . . always grateful . . . .

I chose to be a stay-at-home mom (one of the best choices that I've made) during the first years of our marriage because I didn't want to miss a thing that little Tate did. But, of course, with the choice of staying home, it meant only one income. His job didn't pay very well. We had more bills than we had month and things were about to change again. Robby was notified at work that they were going to have to let some people go. Since he'd been in the last group to be hired, he was laid-off. At this time, we were living in a modest apartment and sharing the only bedroom with our very nocturnal toddler. Our financial status went from little to none! We prayed for another job for Robby and soon he was hired on with another company, thus making our life a little easier since it paid a little more than the last one. We were grateful—and looking back, the layoff was a blessing that we didn't see until later. (We have learned to identify blessings more quickly now.) That month we were not only blessed with the new job, but with the news that our family would be increasing by one. Changes! Changes! Changes!

Everyone knows that a baby changes everything, but we were not aware of just how much the change would challenge our lives. During my pregnancy I found it very difficult keeping up with our very inquisitive toddler, Tate, whose energy level seemed to spike at the most inconvenient times—mostly when I had "morning sickness". (which I kept almost the entire time of pregnancy.) It was during these times that our "energizer bunny" would help himself to my favorite lipstick or climb up to the kitchen sink and turn on the garbage disposal scaring himself into a nervous heap on the floor in the corner of the kitchen. While these were challenging days then, and precious memories now, the really big changes were well on their way!

As the time for our daughter to arrive got closer, I became increasingly aware that I was going to truly have my hands full. Little did I know that the feeling that I was experiencing was a sign to prepare me for what was coming. The labor and delivery had taken almost fifteen hours and in the process my coccyx bone (tail bone) was slowly broken as my daughter prepared to enter this world. I ended up having my child naturally as the pain medications had worn off several hours earlier. It is said that mothers forget the pain of childbirth—I have not. While I am grateful for the program that provided me with prenatal care and delivery, I am happy to now learn that the program has greatly improved. I suffered through many hours of pain and agony to deliver an almost eight pound baby! I was almost three weeks overdue and I am a petite woman of only 5 feet and should have never been allowed to carry the child for that length of time to continue to grow. I do not hold any anger towards the medical staff, but I can't help but to wonder if things would have turned out differently if I had been able to see the same doctor each time. Since the world is full of "what if's", I can only be grateful that God gave me the strength and courage to persevere.

Since the labor and delivery took so long, there was a time that our daughter was without proper oxygen supply. We do not know for how long, but we saw the evidence over the next couple of years. When she finally entered into this world at the end of 1991, she was everything that I had hoped and planned for in all my years of dreaming about that day. She had dark hair, like me and a dimple in her chin like Robby. She was perfectly beautiful. We chose one of the names from my childhood list for her first name and she shares my mother's middle name. I was so exhausted that I don't remember much about what happened next, but Robby said that he was concerned because she was not responding well to the nurses right after delivery. We finally heard her cry enough to satisfy the nurses and I remember an overwhelming sense of relief. It was not until we were home that reality set in.

We took our little bundle home and found that she didn't sleep much at all. Having been around lots of children, I knew that in the early days they slept at least two hours between feedings, but not our daughter. She ate and almost as soon as she fell asleep, she was awake again. I began to feel like I wasn't doing anything right because no matter how many times she ate, was rocked, or changed, she would not stop crying. She even cried when she slept. She cried when she was awake. She cried all the time. For the first two weeks nothing we did stopped the crying. Friends and family offered suggestions and advice. They came to assist us in our time of need—but no one was able to get her settled down. My grandmother suggested that I give her a little watered down baby cereal in her bottle—nothing too much, just enough to fill her tummy. I took her advice and it worked! For the next six hours there was no crying and I began to feel better. Tate was overjoyed too! He asked me in the silence of the afternoon, when that "crying baby" was going to go home! He was not pleased when I informed him that she *was* home—he made the comment that he wished that we'd gotten the "chocolate baby" at the hospital instead! I gave him a big squeeze and we both laughed. He became my comic relief in those early years.

As the days passed, we became aware of the fact that our daughter's feet were turned in toward each other. At the six weeks checkup the doctor stated that it was most likely the cause of being confined in such a tiny space as my tummy without much room to move during those last three weeks. He assured us that it could be corrected. When we mentioned the fact that she was still crying a lot, he excused it away as colic and gave us gas drops. The doctor was happy that she had gained a significant amount of weight and asked what I had been feeding her. When I told him about the watered down cereal he said that was most likely the very reason for all the crying. I tried to explain that it had helped her to sleep and calm down quite a bit from all the crying that she had been doing. It didn't help—the doctor ordered me to stop giving her the cereal and just let her to cry herself to sleep. Well, it has been my experience with children that that does often work, so I agreed to do as he has said. Little did I know that I would be up for almost twenty hours straight with a screaming baby. The tenants in the apartment above us must have been just as miserable. When I couldn't take it any longer, I called the doctor several times during the day and the instructions were always the same: leave her alone and she will eventually cry herself to sleep. I was concerned that something else was wrong when she didn't stop crying after I had checked all the things off the list that could have possibly been the cause of her crying. I thought that perhaps she was just wanted to be held, but that seemed to cause her to cry even more. I quickly took her back in to see the doctor after calling him all day and was met with the his firm belief that I was just being an overly concerned new mother. He assured me that if I would follow his advice, that our daughter would be fine. I returned home, feeling hopeless and defeated. Things begin to improve a little—either that or we just got use to all of the crying—either way, our lives were in constant chaos with very little sleep and even less visitors. We continued to feed her the watered down cereal and the doctor never knew. He never asked and I never mentioned it again.

By the time *LuLu* was eighteen months old she had seen several doctors and none of them could tell me what was causing her mental and developmental delays. He feet were more turned in and we were told to buy her a tricycle to correct her them. The thought was that she couldn't pedal it if her feet were turned in and she would correct them to ride the trike. Although it would be quite some time until she would be ready to operate a tricycle and the battle to keep her from giving up quickly, flying into a crying rage and feeling even more helpless was not even thought about at this time. We prayed for strength and courage and the ability to love and care for this difficult child. I still had faith and trusted God even though I couldn't see any immediate improvements in our daughter. I now understand that I was given extraordinary strength and wisdom by the Father during those years. He used my faith to move many mountains!

As *LuLu* reached her second birthday, we realized that she was mildly delayed in several developmental areas like speech and socialization. Her motor skills were lacking as well. She would often begin the day crawling and then she would stand up to walk a few steps and then she would fall, remaining almost immobile for the rest of the day. Even with assistance standing, she would allow her legs to give way and was satisfied staying in one spot. She did not use words, she simply *growled* at us. She liked to sit alone in the corner rather than join the family at the table. Encouraging her to join us was like trying to bathe a cat! We learned to allow her to sit in her highchair in the corner of the dining room so that we could have a peaceful meal. She was content to sit in the corner and eat with her hands. No matter how hard we tried, she would not use a fork or a spoon. We tried colorful utensils, character utensils and "big girl" utensils—she showed little interest in them as tools by which to use with her food—she would rather use them as projectiles and aimed straight for our faces. I have to admit that her aim was pretty accurate and when she would hit her target, she would let out a deep, almost animal-like laugh that sounded more like a throaty growl. We tried to ignore these events and would not return the utensils to her but this only made matters worse. It would be a long time before she learned how to use a fork and spoon correctly.

I remember on one occasion while we were eating, I tried to show her how to eat with a spoon. The spoon was purple and it changed colors according to the temperature of the food. She seemed mesmerized by this fact and proceeded to busy herself with using the spoon for its correct purpose until the spoon remained the same color for longer than she thought that it should. She quickly began to flail and growl and then she threw the purple plastic spoon straight over the table and hit her older brother right in the middle of the forehead! He was more shocked than hurt. I quickly got up and firmly told her that that kind of behavior was *not* going to be tolerated and I gave her a couple of swats on the backside with a thin paddle ball paddle. She was wearing a diaper, so the swats were more like a shock to her. I was hoping that it would cause her to snap out of it—just the opposite! When I sat her back in the highchair, she kicked at me and then proceeded to pull her hair out in large chunks! I tried my best to get her to stop, but as soon as I got near enough, she latched on to *my* hair and withdrew two fists full of hair from the top of my head! OUCH!

Our family life was in constant chaos as we attempted trips to the park or to the grocery store. While getting ready for such trips, our beautiful daughter would kick and scream and bang her head on the floor, walls or whatever objects were close to her. She would fling herself on the floor and clinch her fists and scream so hard that she turned beet red. Once in the car, her constant moaning irritated us beyond what I can explain. We tried to redirect her attention to the music on the radio or by giving her a favorite toy or blanket. Nothing that we tried appeased her. We were so frazzled by the time that we got to our destination that we couldn't even enjoy it. Her "fits" continued all day and into the night until she would wear herself out and finally fall asleep. The silence in the house was almost deafening—we learned to cherish every moment of it though. Her little sleeping body was so precious—her long eyelashes wet with a mixture of tears and sweat from her lengthy screaming sessions . . . her little round face with her dimpled chin made me want to kiss it. It was very difficult not to scoop up her exhausted body and hold her close and love on her. It just wasn't possible to do since any touching caused her to be over stimulated and thus causing her screaming sessions to ensue once again—we learned that the hard way.

As the days, weeks and months passed, I learned to draw strength from knowing that The Father chose me to be the mother of this very special child. Honestly, it took some time for me to come to this conclusion. I often spent my days in prayer asking God "Why?" rather than feeling honored for being chosen for this role. It took me many years to see things through His eyes. I'm so very glad that He didn't give up on me. I'm very grateful for His patience, grace and love. I never lost my faith in Him, but I did disappoint myself more times than I would care to remember.

By the time *LuLu* was three years old, we celebrated the birth of our new addition—a beautiful little boy that we named Corey. He was so different from our over active Tate (which was now six years old) and our forever fit-pitching *LuLu*. Corey was quiet and still. He had an angelic face and piercing blue eyes like Robby. He played alone quietly in his bed and nothing seemed to cause him distress. He was doted on by big brother Tate but was detested by *LuLu*. We didn't fully understand the magnitude of this feeling until I walked in on her as she was helping me to put Corey to bed one night.

The following is taken from partial entries of my journal pages:

Wednesday, November 16, 1994

LuLu has had a better day today. I'm hoping that since she has turned three she is out of the "terrible twos" stage. She has been such a big helper today! She enjoyed helping me with the laundry. She helped fold the bath cloths and the dish rags and stacked Corey's bibs in a neat pile and we played the matching game with his little socks. But, as we were putting everything away, I heard the toilet flush and I was hoping that she had gone to the bathroom on her own because she's wearing big girl panties now and potty training has been very difficult—especially since Corey has been born. I ran to the bathroom ready to give her an excited and happy hug for her great accomplishment, but what I found was the toilet full of Corey's socks and bibs! She was trying to flush them! She said that she wanted the baby to go bye—bye. The normal tantrum ensued as I fished the items from the toilet and put them into the sink. I tried to calm her down as she was hitting her head on the bathtub each time an article of clothing came out of the toilet. She kept saying, "Baby go bye-bye!" and getting louder with each breath. This scared me but not as much as what I witnessed tonight as we were getting ready to go to bed.

LuLu and Tater had their baths early tonight and I waited until around 7:30 to give Corey his bath. He was usually ready for bed by 8:30 and tonight was no different. As I laid him in his bed and changed him one last time after his bottle, LuLu said, "me help". I liked this idea and I agreed to let her wind up the music mobile that hangs over Corey's crib. She kept saying, "I a big girl!" and "me help!" I thought that this was a good change—especially since the episode earlier today was so aggressive. I allowed her to put the blanket on Corey and turn off the light. We left the room together and went into the living room. She asked for some water before going to bed and I went into the kitchen to get it. When I got back, she was no where to be seen. I called her—no answer. I asked Tate and Robby—they hadn't seen her. I went into my bedroom where Corey's crib is and I found her in the crib laying on top of Corey with a pillow over his face! I started screaming and I asked her what she was doing! She just kept saying, "Baby go bye-bye!" I'm shaking so much right now that I can barely write this! Why does she hate him so much? I spend endless hours with her—reading books, coloring, and singing—while little Corey lays in the playpen. I don't know what to do! Is this what they call sibling rivalry? Tate doesn't seem bothered by the idea that we have another child. Is it because he's gotten use to having LuLu around? But he didn't act like this when she was born—he was so loving to her—when she allowed him to be near her!

I feel so helpless! I don't know what to do! Robby had to put her to bed tonight—I was so distraught that I just couldn't do it! Is this something that I'm going to have to watch all the time? Will she try to do it again? I'm sure that I won't have much sleep tonight. I can hear her kicking the walls and screaming because she doesn't want to go to bed. Poor Tate has to get up early and go to school and the poor little fellow won't get much sleep if she doesn't calm down soon—it's already after 10pm! Lord, please give me the strength to carry on and to help LuLu understand that she is loved just as much as Corey and Tater.

Incidents like this went on for years until Corey could somewhat defend himself. Everyone that I talked with kept ensuring me that it was just sibling rivalry and that it would soon work its way out. It didn't. Things seemed to grow worse. Over the years the attempts to hurt Corey grew in number and in magnitude. I had to have Corey with me all the time because I feared that while I had my back turned, he would be hurt by her. We sang songs about "our loving hands" and how our hands were not meant for hurting one another. We talked about how to be nice and loving. We practiced with baby dolls and stuffed animals. We spent most of the day going over all these things, but to no avail—every time I would turn around, I would hear something bang and Corey cry.

It was during a "mommy and me" time one day that I saw *LuLu* be a loving, caring child. We played "tea party" and laughed at the stuffed animals as I made them pretend to drink our invisible tea. We had a wonderful time! I wish that it could have lasted forever— it didn't! As quick as it came, it went away. The beautiful curls of my daughter's hair were being pulled by her own little hands and her screams were ear piercing! She was on the floor kicking and flailing about—turning our tea set upside down and throwing pieces of it in my direction. I was so confused. I didn't know what had happened to cause such an outburst—it all happened in a blink of an eye! I would soon learn that she could and would change many times throughout the day. We all learned to try our best to keep calm as her tantrums escalated. It seemed if we got upset that her reaction became more intense. We learned to be very consistent with the rules and our expectations of proper behavior even if we felt like we were just talking to ourselves. I have to tell you that these years were lonely, frustrating and depressing for our family. Our interaction with the outside world was very limited and most of our days were lived as though we were prisoners. The days seemed to drag on forever as they turned into weeks, months and eventually years—all the while changes were taking place—not the positive changes that I hoped for. Even though it was difficult to continue to have faith, we persevered because we learned to fully rely on our heavenly Father. I'm so glad that the Father never changes!

> *"Every good and perfect gift is from above,*
> *coming down from the Father of the heavenly lights,*
> *who does not change like shifting shadows".*

James 1:17

Chapter 3

PURPLE PONIES AND SWEET FEET BLANKIES

I bet if you took a minute and thought about your favorite toy from your childhood, a wide smile would spread across your face. Our childhood toys gave us a sense of safety and comfort. As children we are at the mercy of our parents and there are too many parents in this life that seem to make many wrong choices and not thinking of how their choices will affect their children. Our childhood should be a magical time for us—full of wonder and awe—experiencing the world with wide-eyed anticipation and joy—discovering our own independence, while having comforting things to remind us that we are safe.

I had two favorite toys as a child. One was an original, hand-made sock monkey lovingly made for me by my baby sitter, Mrs. Annie Byrd. I watched "Birdie" (as I called her) fashion her husband's socks into the most handsome monkey that my young eyes had ever seen. I named this gift of hand-made love "Monkey"—mispronounced as "Monty"—and that has remained his name all these years. Yes, he's still with me—all tattered and torn and full of childhood memories. I smile when I look at him. His smile brought me much comfort during the lonely days of my childhood and now as I look at him with adult eyes, I am reminded to keep smiling because I'm never alone—the Father has promised to never leave me—I still find comfort in Monty.

My other favorite toy was actually not a toy at all but a small, pink, quilt-like blanket trimmed with a pink, silky border. I can't tell you where I even got the blanket but I remember always having it.

I remember taking it to the first day of school and pretending that it was a magic carpet that would take me to many new and exciting places. I have fond memories of it wrapped around me during some of the scariest parts of my young life. I felt safe with it wrapped around me—surrounding my little shoulders and using the corners of it to dry my tears. I am very thankful for that blanket. It was like the arms of the Father, lovingly wrapped around me bringing me the comfort that I so desperately needed.

Since I was so attached to Monty and my blanket as a young child, it was no surprise that *LuLu* would also share this attachment to her very own blanket and special chosen toy. She was brought home from the hospital in a Carters© Brand blanket with a tiny, little foot print design all over it. She seemed to be the calmest when she was wrapped snuggly in this blanket. As she grew, the blanket became known as the "sweet feet blanket" and never left her side. It was almost impossible to wash it as she would never let it out of her sight and if I tried to quickly wash it while she was asleep, she would wake up before it was dry and go into a screaming panic that would last longer than the drying cycle. Once she got upset, it was very difficult to settle her down again. On a family trip to Florida one year, the sweet feet blankie was left behind and we were half way home when we realized it and had to turn around and go back and get it. How we made it that far without it, I'll never know, but the moment that she was reunited with the blanket, she wiped away her tears with the corners and fell asleep tightly clutching it in her chubby little hands. The sweet feet blankie still remains one of her most prized positions today. She still sleeps with it every night and says that it makes her feel happy and loved. While the blanket has seen better days, I don't think that it could ever be replaced.

We all knew the importance of the sweet feet blankie to *LuLu* but we also knew that she needed other toys too. We learned early on that touch was a very important communication tool with her. She enjoyed soft things and would rub them between her fingers for hours. She was not at all interested in anything that was not soft. She would scream and hit her forehead with her little fists if she was given a toy that didn't pass the softness qualification. This became quite a problem as most of the toys we had were rubbery or plastic and they squeaked or rattled. These kinds of toys made her react aggressively and caused her to fling herself about and bite her fingers and hands. We learned quickly to surround her with the softest toys that we had and to keep all others out of sight as even the sight of them made her react negatively.

There was one exception to the soft rule and it was a purple My Little Pony © pony with a bright pink mane and tail. *LuLu* spotted this at a yard sale and just *had* to have it. I gladly paid the quarter for the toy and was happy to see that she was expanding her toy collection to things other than just the soft items. The purple pony was there at all meals, bath time, and of course bed time. The pony's effect on our little girl was most interesting. We could pretend that the pony would do something and *LuLu* would gladly follow its lead. If we got the pony to lie down and rest at nap time, then she would agree to lay down with it to keep it company. If we pretended that the purple pony was a big girl and used the potty, then she would happily use the potty too. That purple pony was worth so much more to us than the mere quarter that I'd paid. It brought more normalcy to our family than I could even have imagined at that time. Things were going so much better and we used the purple pony to teach her about manners, small chores and lots of other little things.

We were doing so well with all of our daily routines until the day that she had to start school. The sweet feet blankie and the purple pony were not allowed to join her and she didn't like that one little bit! I can't tell you how we made it through those school day mornings other than to say that we were just carried by the Father above. There is no other explanation that I can give because those days were some of the most stressful. There would be more days of chaos ahead, but I think that had I not been given this taste of it at this time, I wouldn't have been able to deal with what was to come. Through this child that the Father blessed me with, I was learning patience and endurance. I was learning to live by faith. I was also learning to love a "difficult to love" person. That, in itself is quite a task and though it was very hard, I was able to see my daughter through the eyes of the Father—as a true blessing.

> *"And let us not lose heart in doing good,*
> *for in due time we shall reap*
> *if we do not grow weary."*

Galatians 6:9

Chapter 4

BATHED IN BUTTER AND SANTA'S SOFT PANTS

I am sure that many parents enjoy sharing the funny things that their children did when they were younger, I know that I do. I see many posts on Facebook © from young mothers that detail the accounts of their little one's musings and mayhem. The social network allows for positive feedback, encouragement and the knowledge that "this time will soon pass and you will miss it" statements from friends. At the time of our wilderness journey, we had nothing like this to encourage us. Our social circle was limited to the members of our church congregation and a few local family members. Although most of them provided encouragement, some of the people in our lives during this time told us that we needed to put her into an institution because she would never be a productive citizen and she would always be nothing more than a nuisance in our lives. I was so hurt by their words. We had gotten the same advice from several of the doctors that we'd seen, but to hear them from our close friends and family, pained us to the core. It seemed like we were on our own with only a handful of friends and family that were willing to help us through this time. Robby and I vowed to each other that we would always be there for each other and that we *were* going to overcome this adversity in our lives with the help of the Father. He put just the right people in our lives to keep us encouraged. While most of those people were only in our lives for a season, the Father used them in great ways to accomplish His purpose for our lives.

One occasion in which we needed a lot of encouragement came when Robby and I overslept one Saturday morning. We had been up all night with *LuLu* because she refused to stop screaming and go to sleep. Even the purple pony was no help this night. She could scream for two hours straight and still seem to have enough energy to kick the walls constantly and throw items around the room. It seemed as if we went into her room to calm her down or to make sure that she wasn't hurting herself, the screaming would escalate. We came to dread bedtime, even though we longed for it, we knew that this was the kind of reaction we were going to get each time. She always acted this way when she didn't want to do what we wanted her to do. Robby and I always stood our ground and never gave in—although there were so many times that we would have been happy to do so just so that we could get a few minutes of peace.

Many friends and family members encouraged us to spank her—stating that that action would straighten her out. I have to say that we did spank—on occasion—as a last resort—and not out of anger. We were almost too exhausted to do much after trying to ensure that she didn't hurt herself during her fits of rage. We realized that there were many people in our lives with all the "answers" but very few of them volunteered to keep her overnight or to take her for any amount of time that would give us a needed break. We were hurt many times by the actions of our circle of friends when it came to matters that concerned our daughter. We understood that they didn't want to get involved because of fear—fear of the unexpected, fear of her hurting herself or their children, fear that they wouldn't know what to do . . . . Robby and I had all the same fears . . . . the only difference was that we had no choice, we felt isolated and ignored by the very people that claimed to be our supporters.

We do not hold any anger or harsh feelings toward anyone that was in our circle of friends during that time and that did not lend a hand. We understand their fears—we only wish that they could have understood ours. We are grateful to those handful of friends that stood by us—lent us their shoulders and their ears as we cried and confessed our feelings of despair.

The following is from a partial excerpt from my personal journal documenting the experience:

Saturday, August 31, 1996

This morning we awoke to the smell of butter. The smell permeated the whole house and since we'd over slept a little we could only image what awaited us as we jumped from our bed and ran into the kitchen. What we found was a sight indeed. I wish that I had my camera to capture the scene. I will do my best to describe it. LuLu was sitting on the floor with the large tub of butter in her lap and Corey was sitting patiently in front of her as if waiting for something. Robby and I watched as she dipped something into the tub of butter and fed it to Corey. It was a raw hotdog covered in butter. Little Corey sat with his mouth open and just waited like a little baby bird ready for another bite. If that wasn't bad enough, as I surveyed the kitchen and looked into the living room, I saw that both our sofa and loveseat were both COVERED in BUTTER! Robby and I were speechless! All I could say is "why?" Everywhere I looked there was butter. There was butter on the front door. There was butter on the mirror in the bathroom and toilet and on the knobs in the bath tub. There was butter on the coffee table and on the t.v screen. There was butter on Corey's almost hairless little head and all over his face. LuLu had butter all over her gown and in her eyelashes and eyebrows. There was butter on the kitchen countertops and the oven door. Butter was smeared on all of the lower kitchen cabinets as well as the door of the refrigerator. The kitchen chairs got their fair share of butter as well as the placemats and table top. Even our poor little kitten, Mr. Socks wasn't immune from the butter bath. His feet and tail was just as greasy as the rest of the house. The cake that I'd made for Corey's birthday celebration today was still in the protective plastic container, but it was all smashed against the sides of it and it was sitting on the top of the butter smeared loveseat. Words cannot explain our feelings at this time. We are at a loss for words. We couldn't save the sofa and loveseat today as they were too far damaged. We will have to look for some more seating and in the mean time, we are sitting on blankets spread across the living room floor. I had to cancel Corey b'day party celebration today because we didn't have a cake or anywhere for anyone to sit. I'm so glad that our neighbors Debra and Paul helped clean up all the butter and haul away the sofa and loveseat. I'm also glad that Corey and LuLu didn't get sick from eating all that butter. I'm still sorry that I didn't have any film for my camera. These are the days that I truly need my mother and God provided a mother-like figure in Debra for me today that dried my tears and encouraged me to smile and see the comedy in it all. Father, thanks for sending me these caring neighbors and for letting me know that I'm not alone on this journey.

With this experience, I've learned some important lessons: 1.) Put the butter in the BACK of the refrigerator 2.) Be very thankful for the helping hands of friends willing to drop everything at a moment's notice and come to my rescue. 3.) To be thankful for the little things—even the days when our house is bathed in butter . . . .

We didn't punish *LuLu* for the butter incident because we weren't sure that she truly understood that what she did was wrong. Her language skills were still lacking and even though she had started school, her comprehension was that of a much younger child. We used the purple pony to help explain that what she did was wrong. It seemed to work as she kept telling us that she was "berry, berry sorry" and that she wasn't going to "look at the butter never again"—her way of telling us that she understood her actions were not acceptable.

Some of my most embarrassing moments came out of this time period. We were on an outing shortly after Corey was born. We were in a local wholesale store and Santa just happened to be greeting everyone as they entered. This poor Santa was dressed in what appeared to be a very old, almost thread-bare suit and he didn't exactly smell of cookies and milk. However, that didn't stop my kids from wanting to visit with him. We told the kids that we would come back and visit Santa after we looked at the toys and had picked out their favorites. It was our plan for me and the kids to visit the toy section while Robby picked up the things that we needed in the grocery department. To tell you the truth, I think that he had the easier job. I had my hands full with all three kids : Tate, 6 years, *LuLu*, 3 years and a newborn Corey. Tate ran from toy to toy and *LuLu* pitched a fit at every toy that I would not allow her to take home that day. I did my best to keep up with the both of them as little Corey lay sleeping in my arms. I knew that I must be crazy to have tried such an outing at a busy season of the year, but it was one of my first real outings after Corey was born and I really needed it.

As we looked up and down the rows of toys and Tate and *LuLu* made their wish lists to tell Santa on the way out, I became overwhelmed with the feelings of panic as I lost sight of *LuLu* amongst the crowd of little children in the toy section. I called for her and she didn't answer—which was not unusual—it was something that we were currently working on but she had not yet mastered it. I called for Tate, who was in deep concentration at the Lego© display. I quickly raced by and grabbed his hand and we began to call for *LuLu* and look for the brightly colored Christmas bow that adorned the top of her little brunette head. As I traveled down one isle and up the next, I saw a glimpse of her running straight for Santa! I tried to cut her off but was not fast enough. By the time I caught up with her, she was standing behind Santa and that's when I saw her take her little, chubby hand and slip it between Santa's legs in a sawing motion—she "sawed" all the way to the front of Santa in a swift motion and then back again. By the time I reached for her arm, she giggled and ran off—leaving me with my hand at the level of Santa's back side just as he turned around! He smiled a wide smile and gave a hefty belly laugh and said, "Ho Ho Ho little lady!"—I stood there frozen and shaking my head and I kept repeating, "No, No, No . . . it was my *daughter* . . . she likes soft things and she just wanted to feel your soft pants . . . ." I was so embarrassed!! This *has* to be the most embarrassing thing that ever happened to me. It's funny *now* and I like to share it, but at the time I wanted to run and hide because not only did Santa think that I had done this deed, so did all those who were waiting around the door where he was standing. I imagine that countless security camera operators were on the floor laughing too! Even after all these years, I have not set foot into that store again. I'm sure that I will one day, but I'll tell you that I haven't made any plans to do so in the near future—especially at Christmas time!

Chapter 5

BY THE LIGHT OF THE MOON

Most of this chapter will contain some very personal journal entries during the middle of our wilderness journey. There is a lot of pain, fear and sadness in the content. I tried to always include a written prayer or offer some sort of "silver lining" to the end of each entry—I wasn't always successful. It is my hope that through these writings that you will truly see how the hand of God brought us out of this "wilderness" and into witnessing a true miracle. Those that know *LuLu* today will not recognize the child that I describe in the journal entries below and for that, I'm forever thankful to the Father.

The following pages are partial entries from my personal journal that I kept solely on my experiences with our daughter. They span several years and many of the names and dates have been changed to protect the innocent and guilty alike. I will start with the first entry after we moved to Millbrook, Alabama.

August 1999

I have some good news to share! We have just purchased our first house! I do hope that this is a sign that things will continue to improve for our family. The house is in Millbrook, Alabama and it belonged to Robby's grandmother, Gran Becky. Robby spent many of his childhood days in this house and we are thrilled to be able to make some lasting memories with our own children here.

I have decided to continue to write about our life with LuLu. Most of my writings have been on plain notebook paper but when I was given this beautiful journal by my mother in law, I decided to put it to good use! I will do my best to describe most of our days together and try and stay as positive as possible. In the past, I have not been so disciplined. I will make it a point to stay as optimistic as I can be while still documenting all the details of our daily life together. I know that with God ALL things are possible and I plan on being victorious through Him. I'm ready for a miracle—I have not lost my faith—I'm still believing . . . .

This is a new start for all of us. We are enjoying the neighborhood with its nicely manicured lawns and the friendly faces that pass us each day. We are able to get out and ride our bikes and have little squirrels run through the yards and up the trees as we pass by each house on our block. We've enrolled the kids in school and they seem to like it—even LuLu has made a slight change in her attitude about school. She is now in the first grade and I pray that she will learn quickly to be social and deal with her anger issues in a positive way. I pray that I can remain strong and that I can find some help for her. She's so loving at times—yet, so hateful at others. I pray for wisdom in my relationship with her. Thank you Father for giving us a fresh start.

September 26, 1999

Today has been full of anger and stress. We attempted to visit a local church this morning and LuLu screamed during the first part of the service because I wouldn't let her have anymore of the mints from my purse. She slipped off the pew and onto the floor and began to kick the pew in front of us. I tried to collect her as quickly as I could and leave without further incident but that just didn't happen. LuLu refused to walk and all I could do was drag her by her arm out of the sanctuary while she screamed at the top of her lungs. I could hardly walk as she kicked and twisted. Anyone in the path of her feet and legs was fair game and all I could do was apologize over and over again. I don't even remember the ride home or how I was able to collect all the kids and get them all buckled into the car. I will not try to visit another church without Robby again—or if I do, I will try it alone for my sanity and for the benefit of those that are trying to worship in the house of the Lord. I know that there is a church home for us somewhere out there. I pray for an understanding church family to support and encourage us as we travel through our time in the "wilderness".

September 27, 1999

Today has been a wonderful day for LuLu! She got up in plenty of time to eat breakfast and she dressed herself—even her shoes were on the correct feet! She sat patiently as I brushed her soft hair and she didn't fuss about her hair bow. She sat and ate her breakfast quietly and I thought that I saw a smile creep across her face more than once. Oh how I wish that everyday could be this pleasant. I wish that I could capture this moment in time and relieve it over and over again. I hope that this is a sign that things are going to get better. It's great to be happy—it's been such a long time since I've had this kind of peace—true peace that surpasses all understanding—I feel that there are so many more good things to come! I can't wait to see what the Lord is going to do in LuLu's life. I know that He has a great purpose for us all and I know that she is no exception.

October 31, 1999

Tonight we all dressed up and went out to several fall festivals at several local churches. LuLu and I dressed up as black cats. She had a ribbon collar with a little bell on it and she was dressed in a black leotard and black tights. She had little black kitten ears with tufts of black feather-like fur around the edges of them. She also had a long, black tail that we pinned to the back of her leotard. Her little black, fleece bedroom shoes completed the outfit and she looked just darling. I was surprised to have her sit still enough for me to quickly paint on her little black nose and her long whiskers on her little face. The whole outfit was just precious—the pictures don't do it justice. Tate was dressed as a pirate complete with eye patch and plastic sword. We were able to find a fake beard and mustache and he wore them most of the time—although about half way through our night, they ended up in my hands because they were no longer comfortable to him—who could blame him—they were very itchy.(Yes, I tried them on!) Corey was dressed as a Dalmatian puppy—complete with large, black, floppy ears that I sewed myself and a painted on black nose. I made the ears so that they would fit under his 101 Dalmatians hat because I knew that he wouldn't take it off. His little fleece suit was white with spots on it and it had a cute little tail attached in the back that moved a little from side to side when he walked. The outfit was completed with his little 101 Dalmatians tennis shoes that he got for his birthday. (the hat and the shoes came together as a set) Robby joined us by dressing up as the McDonald's Hamburgler© which made us all laugh. He completed his outfit with a squeaky cheeseburger toy (dog toy) but he refused to wear the big black shoes that went with the costume and chose to wear his white tennis shoes instead—even still, the sight of him in that suit was hilarious. Every time someone looked his way, he would

*squeeze the hamburger toy and say, "Rubble, Rubble!"
which sent us all into fits of laughter. It was turning out
to be a great night. LuLu had done quite well and she had
even shared her candy with the boys. I was amazed at the
difference in her today. I was sure that this was a good
sign of better days to come . . . .*

*. . . But, after our outings tonight, we decided to go
through the drive-through at McDonald's © so that Robby
could show off his costume. Everyone in the restaurant
laughed when they noticed us drive by. We ordered five
cheese burgers (one for each of us) and made our way
out of the drive-through to head home. "LuLu" began
to scream and kick the back of Robby's seat when she
realized that we weren't going to stay at the restaurant.
She was screaming so loud that she couldn't hear me
explain to her that we were taking the burgers home to
eat them. The boys begged her to be quiet and tried to
explain that she was going to get to eat when she got
home. Nothing seemed to get the point across to her. We
stopped the car and Robby told her that if she didn't stop
screaming and kicking that she wasn't going to get her
burger at all. This sent her into a more powerful tantrum
because it was as if she just heard only the part about not
getting her burger at all. It was a long ride home. While
the restaurant was only about two miles from our house,
it seemed to take forever to get home.*

*As I opened the doors to get everyone out of the car,
she continued her tantrum. Her cute little cat face paint
was smeared and wet with sweat and tears. Her hands
were covered in some of the paint and she wildly grabbed
her hair and pulled at it. By the time we all got into the
house, she had wet her pants and her face and fingers
were bleeding from all the hitting and biting herself. I
quickly wrestled her into the tub and dried her off and got*

her into her purple pony pajamas. She ran into the kitchen and got up to the bar and patiently awaited her burger like NOTHING had happened. I feel like I'm in the twilight zone! One minute she is an angelic, very well-behaved child and the next she is out of control like a wild animal! I know that my sweet little girl is in there somewhere—I pray for wisdom in my relationship with her.

Additional entry:

It's 3am and LuLu is screaming at the top of her lungs! The whole house is awake! The boys are sitting beside me in the living room as I write this. I feel that I have to write something or I will certainly burst! I feel so helpless! She is punching the air and growling and crying. I went in there to check on her when I first heard her screams. She looked like she was fighting someone. I guess that I got too close and her fist hit me right in the nose causing it to bleed. I know that she didn't do it on purpose, but she's already broken my nose one with her tantrums. I know that this may not be a tantrum, but sometimes I am scared to be in the same room with her sometimes! Why can't I think of something to do to help her? Why can't I be a better mom? I'm so angry with myself! I refuse to let her go through life like this! I will seek more help for her! God, Father, please help me—help me to help my little girl—please help me to get my sweet little girl back!

November 1999

LuLu has celebrated another birthday this month. She doesn't seem to be improving much. We are looking into some outside counseling this next year. I hope that we can find some source of assistance.

December 1999

It's almost the year 2000! Everyone has been saying that at midnight tonight, or computers are going to shut down and everything is going to go bezerk. We will see. It's now about 10pm and I'm making hot chocolate for everyone. We've just met our new neighbors and they have a daughter who just happens to be celebrating her birthday <u>tonight</u>! I hope that this little girl will be a good friend to LuLu as they are about the same age. Thank you Father for sending us some neighbors and a possible best friend for her.

Jan. 1ˢᵗ, 2000

We made it to the year 2000 without any computer failure! LuLu is playing at our new neighbor's house and the feeling that I have is so hard to explain! I'm so happy to have some sort of normalcy in my life. I know that LuLu needs a friend that will understand her and that can help her learn the social graces that she needs to know!

June 2000

It's been several months since my last entry. Much has changed. LuLu has completed 1ˢᵗ grade and will be going into the 2ⁿᵈ grade at a different school. I am concerned that this transition will not be a smooth one as she doesn't adjust to change very well. I am concerned that she will not know how to connect with another school counselor. Ms. D. was great with her and I wonder what obstacles this new school year will bring.

LuLu seems to be very down lately—more than usual. She and the neighbor girl don't really get along that well. They are so very different. The neighbor girl seems so . . .

35

well, I guess the word that I'm looking for is MATURE. It seems as though she more of the age of Corey (6) rather than her own age of 9. At times, she seems much younger than Corey. We are still having problems with her wetting her pants. I've taken her to the doctor and they says that she doesn't have any medical issues that would be causing her problems. I have to remember to be patient and loving and try to understand her.

I have found that many things irritate LuLu. She doesn't seem to understand the concept of sharing or fair play. She's very demanding of others and she's hurtful with her words and lies. She is beginning to steal also. She has come home this last school year with items that weren't hers. I've been working with her teachers and counselor, Ms. D. and I have simply returned the items to the school each day. Her teacher ensured me that she would give them back to the rightful owners. The stealing has not happened too often—the problem is that it's happening at all!

August 2000

Summer is over! Summer vacation is over and the kids have all started back to school. LuLu seems to be well-adjusted to the idea of going to a new school. I've met her new teacher, Ms. Sims and she seems very sweet. She assured me that she would get to see the school counselor, Ms. Emily at least <u>twice</u> a week. I'm so very thankful!

LuLu still cannot grasp the concept of time. I'm still using the phrases: "when the sun comes up" for day time and "when the sun goes down" for night and "cartoon day" for Saturdays. We sometimes say "when the sun goes to bed, so do you!" These things have worked so far but, it's been our experience that many things don't last for long—it's like she gets bored with things—but then again, she likes to have a steady routine. I pray that I can continue to be strong and help her to be all that God created her to be!

September 2000

LuLu seems to be having a good time in school. Although she realizes that she is different from the other kids. I often see her play out her interaction with the classmates in her room at night. She lines up her stuffed animals and dolls and she picks one to be her—it's always ths same one—she tries to "play" with the other "children" but they say mean things to her—she expresses her hurt feelings, but they don't seem to care. She makes her stuffed animal self run away and cry. The stuffed animal "children" are made to "laugh" at her. When I saw this, I began to cry! I went into her room and I asked her why she was playing like that. She leaned over and said, "LuLu is NOT smart or pretty like the other girls! She is DUMB and UGLY! NOBODY likes her!" I tried to suggest that maybe she'd simply misunderstood some of the little girl's actions—she quickly shook her head in protest and replied, "I don't want to live like this anymore!" I have no idea what she meant. I contacted Ms. Sims and she said that speak to the little girls in her class about their behavior and encourage them to include her in their play. Ms. Sims also suggested a meeting with Ms. K. Abernathy, a school coordinator of some type. Whatever helps my daughter, I'm all for it!

September 2000

I'm in pain—my heart is broken! I just met with K. Abernathy and was told that some tests had been given to LuLu and the tests results showed that she is borderline *mentally retarded! WHAT? What does that mean? Why do I feel so ashamed? Is this my fault? I'm so very scared! What can I do? Will she ever get better? I'm shaking so bad! What does all this mean? I feel so alone! I know that she must feel so alone too! How can I help her? I must be strong and have faith—we WILL make it through this—we WILL~ Oh, I love you LuLu! I'm so sorry that I didn't know! I know that I may have gotten on to you for things that you didn't even know that you were doing wrong! I wish that I could go back to the beginning and understand you better! I will try harder to understand you now and in the future—why you act out like you do. I promise to have more patience and to try more positive ways to handle your outbursts. I'm so sorry that I got on to you for wetting your pants all this time—you probably couldn't help it. I love you so very much!*

October 2000

Since my last entry, I have gathered my strength and courage from the Father and I'm willing to face the fact that my child does indeed have a problem—it's not a behavioral problem—it's a mental/emotional problem. My goal now is to find a solution to help her to be a productive citizen. I have spent many hours on my face before the Lord and I know that journey will not be an easy one. I know that He will give me the wisdom that I need to help put our family back together. I have decided to continue to document all the behavior and my response to her as we travel on this journey together. I refuse to feel helpless anymore! I am strong in the Lord and I'm very blessed with many great gifts from the Father—especially my little LuLu. I will overcome each hurdle and be victorious in all aspects in dealing with her with the help of the Father.

November 2000

LuLu seems not to need much sleep anymore! It's almost as if she's on constant "recharge". I try hard to keep up with her—it's hard and I'm exhausted! My response so far has been begging and pleading with her to go to sleep! This has NOT been successful!! I have tried sleeping with her—rewarding her for going to sleep, applying a consequence for NOT going to sleep, refusing to allow her to "catch up" on her sleep in the weekends—all of these have failed! I will be trying a mood light and some music. I found a light at K-Mart that has little squares on it that changes colors gradually—it's very soothing. I've placed it in "LuLu"'s room and she is very happy! I've also gotten a classical music cd for babies. She seems to really enjoy both of these things! I have allowed her to be the one to turn these items on each night before bed. This has really seemed to help get her in the bed and keep her there. Within 20 minutes, she is fast asleep. I don't know who thought of the color changing light, but I'm very thankful for them! Thank you Father for allowing me to find the light and the music and providing me with the funds to obtain them!

November 2000

LuLu has been very upset the past few weeks. Her birthday has come and gone. She seems to be very sad and she hardly ever smiles. I have decided to implement: Girl Time! Just me and my little LuLu—no one else. We use this time to paint our finger nails, read books to each other, watch a movie and eat popcorn, play with Barbies or bake some cookies. This seems to work GREAT! Although, I don't wait until she has been sad for a while—I usually plan for Girl Time at least once a week. We both look forward to this time together. I don't know who's more excited—me or her! I know that this is a definite KEEPER response!

December 2000

LuLu is continuing to have outrageous tantrums! She continues to hit her head on the walls, floors, furniture, or whatever is in sight! In the past, I have taken the advice from other mothers to allow her to stay in her room and scream and get her tantrum over with, but it didn't work for me. When I allowed her to do that, she screamed for 3 hours straight! My head felt like it was going to explode! I will not be going through that again! I decided to try the swaddling action that another mother told me about. She told me that it works for her daughter (who is going through the terrible 2's) and that maybe it would work for us too. Well, I found out quickly that it DOES NOT work for us! When I went in and wrapped the blanket around her to swaddle her, she became more violent! She thrashed about so much that she ended up breaking my nose for the second time! I was sitting on the floor with her wrapped up in by lap. She was flinging herself against my chest with all her might. I was telling her how much I loved her and how I knew that she could settle down and breathe . . . then it happened! Her head flew back and smacked me square in the nose! Oh the pain! I ended up going to the doctor and he confirmed my fear—it was indeed broken! There's not much you can do for a broken nose so, he just placed a butterfly bandage on it! I will NOT even consider the swaddling technique anymore! I'm trying something new this week. I've been reading about children with emotional needs. It has been suggested in the reading material to encourage the children to breath in order to control their emotions—including anger. Guess what? This technique really works! It's a true keeper! It's almost like LuLu forgets to breathe when she gets into one of her tantrums. I've stood in her room and calmly told her that it would be okay and that she needed to breathe. It worked very well and the tantrum only lasted a little over an hour! I'll trade that time for the usual 3-4 hours that it usually is! Praise the Lord!!

Additional entry:

LuLu was very upset tonight when it was time to go to bed. Even the thought of turning on the color changing light and the cd didn't beckon her to her bed. She threw her usual tantrum—throwing items across the room, screaming, banging her head on the walls, floor, etc. I simply walking in her room very calmly and said the following: LuLu, I love you very much and I feel very sad when you're upset like this. I don't like to see you hurt yourself and break your things. I understand that you are angry that your day is over and now you have to go to bed. But, did you know that you are growing as you sleep? God has made everything and everything must have time to grow. I know a story of a little flower that grew into such a beautiful flower that everyone who sees it smiled and thanked God for its beauty and wonderful smell. I even think that it had its own song. Would you like to hear it?" By this time, she had quieted down because I was speaking so softly that she had to stop to be able to hear me. She simply nodded her head and with great interest she crawled back on her bare bed as all the covers had been pulled off and were lying in a tangled mess on the floor. I sang this little song to her: "Grow up! Grow up! Grow up everything! Grow up flower, grow big and tall, grow up flower, don't stay small. Grow up flower, grow big and sing! Grow up flower, for God made everything!" She asked for me to sing it again and I did, but instead of saying the word FLOWER, I said "LuLu". She really liked it! I spent about 30 minutes in her room and we worked together getting her covers back on her bed. I didn't get on to her for the mess in her room—it wasn't even mentioned. I ended up with a short prayer (as usual) but this time I added: LuLu, just like that little flower in our song, you have to grow so that you can share your beauty and make people smile. You have to go to sleep because that's how you grow. I have to bed and so does Dad and your brothers! Now, just breathe and know that everyone is sleeping now. It's time for all little girls and flowers too to go to sleep". It WORKED! Within 15 minutes, she was ASLEEP!!! I thank the Father for giving me a calm spirit even though she was screaming so very loud. Because I whispered, she had to get quiet to hear what I was saying! I'm smiling—inside and out! I think that the flower story and the song will be with us for many days to come! Praise the Lord!!! YES!!

December 2000

Well, this year has almost gone! I've tried to keep positive and keep using the things that work with LuLu. This week has been really hard. It's the last week before school ends for Christmas break. She still has no concept of time and the phrases "when the sun comes up/goes down" are not helping today. She got very frustrated this morning when she was getting ready for school. She took forever to get her clothes on. It took her over 30 minutes to put on one sock! She kept taking it off and putting it back on! Then she would switch and place the sock on the other foot. When I tried to help her, she got very angry and began biting herself. I stopped helping and told her that she would have to hurry and do it herself if she didn't want my help. I made a sing-songy rhyme out of it: "Hurry! Hurry! Don't be slow! Hurry! Hurry! It's time to go! Hurry! Hurry! We can't be late! It's time for school and I can't wait!" She kept saying this and it helped her to focus on the task of getting her socks and shoes on.

Fixing her hair was a different story. I usually let her hold the hair scrunchy and a small mirror so that she can see what I'm doing to her hair—but yesterday she threw the mirror down on the floor and shattered it because she wanted to wear a different bow in her hair. Since we had no mirror this morning, I decided to ask her to sing the "grow up flower" song. She did and then she replaced the word FLOWER with each of our family members. It was the perfect amount of time to get her hair fixed and ready to walk out the door! Thank you Father for little bits of wisdom—the little songs are perfect! I'm no great singer, but I understand that LuLu relates well to music and song. Thank you Lord for this revelation!

December 2000

Christmas has come and gone for this year. I've enjoyed spending time with the kids and Robby. I have to say that most days have seemed like they would NEVER end as far as dealing with LuLu. If she didn't get her way or something made her feel slighted in any way, she would begin to flail herself on the floor and hit her head on the walls and floor. Often we are at a loss to know exactly WHAT sets her off. We can be watching a movie and then, all of a sudden she begins to growl and kick her feet. Most of the time we are just walking on egg shells around her. I do not like it when she asks for things that she can't have (like more ice cream) because I know that she will be having a tantrum that will last for the remainder of the day. These past few days after Christmas has just been almost unbearable. I know that the boys will be glad to return to school. I guess that I can't blame them! Robby and I have told them that they DO NOT have to share their new items with LuLu if they don't want to. We had an incident last month where she decided to break several items that belonged to the boys that she was told that she couldn't play with. We have toys that the kids are required to share and then we have the toys that they don't have to share unless they want to. Poor little Corey offered to share his toy with her and she ended up throwing it against the wall, causing it to break. (It was the remote to a remote control jeep that he got for his birthday in September) I don't know what to do anymore! Father, please give me more wisdom in this area.

January 2001

School has started back and the daily routine continues to drain me. LuLu continues to have more and more bad dreams. She describes them in such detail—horrible monsters, strangers . . . "bad men" . . . she stresses out a lot especially when bed time is close— the flower song and the color changing light box is not helping—nor is the classical music! This is a definite problem that needs a solution fast!!

January 2001

LuLu is continuing to wet her pants. I took her back to the doctor for more testing and they found NOTHING wrong with her. The doctor said that she is just a strong willed child that doesn't take time out to go to the bathroom and waits until the very last minute—and then, it's too late. Her pants are wet several times a day and she smells so awful that we don't want to be around her. We've done several things to help her with this problem without much success.

At this particular time, I always have an extra set of clothes with us at all times along with a plastic garbage bag and a towel for her to sit on in the car. I have started making her responsible for washing her own underwear and pants in the washing machine. But I fear that she is getting too much enjoyment out of operating the washing machine! We've just recently implemented the deal that if she goes 2 days (we mark them on a calendar in her room) without wetting her pants, she get to go to the Dollar Tree and get ONE item of her choice. This has been successful so far. The plan is to continue to lengthen the days gradually—from 2 days to 4 days and then a week. Praying that this works!

January 2001

LuLu has been complaining about stomachaches, headaches, ear aches, and backaches. She asked me today is she could use the crutches that she saw in our closet. When I denied her request, she flew into a rage and screamed that she hated me! Her tantrum lasted about an hour and a half. She locked her door after I went in to try and calm her down with the breathing technique. I couldn't even get the first few words out before she was throwing things at me. I told her that that was not acceptable behavior and she came at me aggressively and told me in a low, almost growling voice to get out! She then locked the door and we heard things breaking and heard her hitting the walls with her head and fists. All I could do is sit and pray! I feel so very helpless! I don't know what to do!!

January 2001

We watched the <u>Left Behind</u> movie at church tonight. LuLu has cried and held onto me sooo very tight! She *continues to beg me not to die. She keeps telling me that she doesn't want to die either! Poor thing! I didn't know it would affect her like this—if I did, I would not have allowed her to watch it. I tried to get her to go to the nursery/children's department with the other kids, but she kept sticking out her tongue at one of the little girls that was walking by when the Pastor dismissed the younger kids. I knew that if I insisted, I would have my hands full. Robby was not with us tonight, so I had to deal with her the best way that I could. I allowed her to sit with me, but now I wish that I'd just stayed at home. She has refused to leave my side for the last hour and I feel that I may have to sleep in her room tonight—which is fine, but I wish that I had just made this night a family night in at home!*

January 2001

LuLu has started taking things that do not belong to her again. We were visiting some friends tonight and we let the kids all play together in the play room. We all had a good time and every one had a great attitude when it was time to leave—even my little LuLu! I couldn't believe it! I was proud! I kept praising her in the car for her good choices but was very disappointed when we got home and found message on our answering machine from the friend that we had just visited. In short, the message was that her little girl was missing her favorite stuffed animal and then she described it. Her little girl could be heard crying in the background. I thought to myself that surely this beloved toy was just misplaced—after all, LuLu had not taken things in a very long time—I went to ask her about it in hopes that my thoughts were correct. I found the beloved toy of my friend's daughter hidden in her pillow case. When I asked her about it, she began to scream and hit me. She said that we don't love her and that we never let her have anything! I told her to look around her room and see all the nice things that she had. I told her that she had more nice things, but that she CHOSE to break them. Hearing this sent her into a rage and she grabbed the coveted stuffed animal and began to tear it apart. It was a Beanie Baby and all the beans flew everywhere! Almost immediately, as if a light switch had been flipped, she began to cry uncontrollably. She hugged me and continuously apologized for her actions. She kept hitting her forehead with her fists and saying: "I'm soooo STUPID! I HATE ME! I HATE being ME!" I held her in my lap for a long time and I rubbed her hair and hummed a little song. This is very unusual for her to be remorseful! I have hope that she is beginning to understand more. Thank you Father for this time of peace. Thank you for giving me the strength and the wisdom to handle this situation. I pray for the finances to replace the Renee's toy. I pray for forgiveness and understanding from my friend and her family and that this incident won't place a strain on our friendship.

February 2001

Yesterday was an almost perfect day! But that is NOT the case today! From the time LuLu got up this morning she has been very grouchy! It started on her way to the bathroom. Corey jumped out of his doorway to scare her and she screamed and shoved him backwards into the railing of his metal bunk beds. Corey sat on the floor crying and holding his head and LuLu went on about her business of using the bathroom and going into the kitchen for her breakfast. She never gave Corey or the incident another thought until I found out what happened and asked her why she did it—I don't bother asking IF she does things anymore—I KNOW that she does them— Corey's little head was bleeding and she sat eating her cereal like nothing had happened! When I asked her

WHY she had pushed Corey, she replied that it was just because he wouldn't leave her alone! When I tried to explain that he had done nothing to her but try to play with her by scaring her on her way to the bathroom, she rolled her eyes and told me to leave her alone! I told her that she was not going to get to finish her cereal until she apologized to Corey for what she had done and I took her cereal from in front of her. She jumped up and screamed at me and went to hit Corey who was standing nearby. I immediately stepped in front of her and threw the cereal in her face. I didn't do it intentionally—it was a reflex. I have to say that it stopped her in her tracks and she began to cry. She began to apologize to me and Corey and we all worked together to clean up the cereal mess. I didn't apologize for throwing the cereal in her face, but I did tell her that I was sorry that I had to do it—that I felt like she gave me no other choice. She seemed to understand and when we got everything cleaned up she asked to take a bubble bath with her Barbies—sounded like a great idea to me! While she was in the tub, our neighbor's daughter came over and asked if LuLu could play. I told her that she could as soon as she got out of the tub. When she heard about her invitation to play, she quickly jumped out of the tub, happily got dressed and ran next door.

The play date didn't last long! LuLu was only gone for about 30 minutes when she came stomping in the door with her fists clinched and looking for items to break. According to LuLu, the little girl next door refused to let her play with a particular item in her playhouse and that's when LuLu tried to push her out of the playhouse. The playhouse is built off the ground—sort of like a free-standing tree house without the tree. The neighbor girl was yelling and crying and begging her not to push her off the playhouse porch. When her mother came out and saw what was happening, she told LuLu to come home. I was about to ask her my usual WHY when the neighbor and her daughter appeared on my back patio. She wanted an apology from LuLu for her actions but she boldly refused and shouted several hateful words at the mom and the daughter. I was so very embarrassed! I told the neighbors that I was so sorry and that they would get an apology soon. As they went to leave, I heard a loud crash! I ran to see what it was and I saw that LuLu had pulled down her closet door! (It is the wooden, sliding kind that hangs on a series of little wheels and fits onto a small railing) The wheels at the top of the door were bent and the door had fallen away from the closet causing many things in its path to be broken. I am at another loss! Robby had to work today and I'm dealing with this all alone! I'm so upset! I don't know what to do! Father, please let us find someone to help us soon! I don't know how much more of this I can take!

February 2001

Well, needless to say that LuLu will not be playing with our next door neighbor any time soon. It seems that the incident last week was too much for them. Even though she did finally apologize last week, they made it very clear that they were not interested in any more play dates with her. This was very hard for me to take.

I found out today that LuLu told another neighbor across the street that Robby and I are always fighting and that we yell and scream at each other. This couldn't be farther from the truth! I was shocked when the neighbor met me at the mailbox and asked if I was okay and began to tell me of her concerns. I didn't know what to say! I told her that LuLu must have misunderstood something. I assured her not to worry that we were all doing fine and that my relationship with Robby is just fine!

When I asked LuLu what she had told the neighbor about me and Robby fighting, she sat and looked at me with a kind of cold look and said that she told the TRUTH about us! That someone needed to know that we fight all the time! I tried to get her to name a time that she saw or heard us fighting, but she said that I know that she was telling the truth. I told her that I didn't know what she was talking about and then she got a terrible attitude—she crossed her arms, rolled her eyes and said, "Yes, I KNOW that you love each other and it makes me SICK! I don't want to see you kiss!" And then she began to laugh. I was so confused! In just a matter of minutes she went from being angry to being almost silly!

I was hoping that she had outgrown this stage. She had done this before when she was in kindergarten. She told her teacher and the school counselor that the bruise that she had on her thigh was from where Robby had punched her with his fists—even though they were actually from a fall on her bicycle. (She was learning how to ride her bike without the training wheels—we had just taken them off) She turned too sharp and fell in some gravel in a neighbor's driveway. The handlebars had turned and the grips had made little bruises on her chubby little legs. I had four witnesses and three of them were adults. She had decided to tell her teacher that Robby had hit her because he told her that she couldn't go home with a classmate that particular afternoon and she'd gotten mad at him for not allowing her to go. The teacher told the campus police officer and we soon found ourselves under investigation. I tried to explain that the bruises were no way from Robby and that the marks matched the handlebar grips and that he was welcome to come and check it out for himself. I explained that LuLu gets upset easily and that this was probably the case that day. He didn't seem to believe me but he decided to check with the neighbors whose names and contact numbers I'd given him. I never heard from the officer again and all the neighbors that got a call said that they confirmed my statement that she did fall on her bike and that they noticed the bruises almost right away. They also told the officer that there was no way that Robby could have made those bruises as his hands are a lot wider than the small grips on the handlebars. I guess that the officer believed them, After that, the teacher looked at us very differently. We had a meeting with school officials shortly after this incident and the teacher told us that she had asked LuLu about her home life each day and that they were very concerned about her well-being. I finally had to pull her out of the Brewbanks school and homeschool her for the second half of kindergarten. (This was her 2nd year in kindergarten)

February 2001

LuLu got into a BIG fight with Corey this morning! He was the first in line for the bus. She can't stand not being first, and she has a hard time sharing—anything: toys, me and any attention. She pulled Corey's jacket (the hat part) and ripped it. She flung Corey on the ground and got on the bus leaving him crying and his hands and knees scraped up. Tate helped him up and brought him back into the house. I got him all cleaned up and I took him and Tate to school. The bus driver called when I got back home from taking them and told me that LuLu had screamed and hit the back of the seat all the way to school. She went on to tell me that LuLu wouldn't be allowed to ride anymore if this kind of behavior continued. I don't know what I'm going to do with her! How do I approach this issue? Lord, please help me to have the courage and the strength to overcome this.

February 2001

Today we were on our way to the library and the park. But, I stopped by the gas station to get gas first, and LuLu LOST it! She got soooo upset because I didn't tell her of this plan before we stopped at the gas station! I will work harder on trying to prepare her for our plans and we will work together on the unexpected things that come up that we can't plan for. I do hope that this will work!

*LuLu had another tantrum when I told her to do some of her chores. She huffed, stomped, growled—it took her over three hours to simply make her bed and put away her clothes. I have tried to help, but it makes matters worse. I have decided to make a list of all the things that needed to be done around the house and let her choose a chore and then mark it off when the task is completed. **UPDATE NOTE**: This is a KEEPER technique! This seems to work very well. I only hope that it lasts!*

March 2001

*I went to check on LuLu tonight as she was getting ready for bed and I noticed that she had several Band-Aids on her fingers. I decided against my better judgment and asked her about them. She said she had them on her fingers because they were bleeding! I asked her if I could look at one of them and it appeared that she had bitten her fingernails down too far causing her fingers to bleed. I wrapped it back up and told her that tomorrow we would put some pretty polish on them to help remind her not to bite her nails. She seemed to like the idea! I hope that this is another keeper technique! **UPDATE NOTE**: This is a KEEPER technique! We've been doing this for the last couple of weeks and it's working very well. She is still biting them, but not as much! I'll take it!*

March 2001

Okay, so I've documented some of the keeper techniques that I've used with LuLu and I think that I've found one that will work for all three kids! It's called: The Penny System; and I came up with it while I was crying and praying by the light of the moon last night. We live in a world that pays those that work—and chores are a type of work—so why not reward the kids for the chores that they do? I hope that this works! The kids will collect pennies for tasks that they perform each day. The kids will earn pennies as a symbol of payment and they will use the pennies to pay for privileges such as watching t.v. and playing video games. They will also have to pay consequence fee for rules broken such as talking back or hitting. In the future, as our Penny System becomes the norm, I will add additional items as the kids grow.

Here's the way that I've worked this out:

THE PENNY SYSTEM

	Chore (we all help)	Pay in Pennies	Privileges (things that you get to do)	Privilege Prices
Hygiene	Brushing teeth	*1 each time (3 max)*	Popcorn	*10*
	Brushing hair	*1 (in morn. & when needed)*	Candy (after meals)	*10*
	Washing hands	*2 before meals*	T.V. Time (30 min.)	*15*
	Getting dressed	*2 (clothes must be clean)*	Video game (30 min.)	*15*
	Bath/shower	*4 (every day)*	Computer time (30 min.)	*15*
			Chocolate milk (when avail)	*20*
Positive Character	Smile	*3 (with feeling & not asked)*	High tea time	*20*
	Sharing	*3 (freely & when reminded)*	Movie (when available)	*25*
	Hugs	*3 (given freely)*	Telephone (15 mins)	*25*
	Good Manners	*4 (at home & away)*	Playing outside (30 mins)	*30*
	Good attitude	*4 (at home & away)*	Play date w/ friend	*50*
	Acts of Kindness	*4 (without being told)*	Rainy day box item/ activity	*50*

54

	Loving words	***4*** *(without being told)*	*Park visit (when available)*	***60***
	Going to bed on time	***4*** *(with good attitude)*	*Spend the night company*	***100***
	Getting up on time	***4*** *(with good attitude)*	*Spend the night away*	***100***
	Telling the truth	***4*** *(freely & when reminded)*	*You name it . . . .*	***150***
School	*Homework*	***2*** *(with good attitude-try)*		
	Good note	***3*** *(from teacher/ coach)*		
	Tests/Grades	***3*** *(tried best)*		
	Behavior	***4*** *(no problems at school/bus)*		
Help with Household	*Dusting*	***1*** *(any room-after Hoovering done)*		
	Straighten Pillows	***1*** *(on sofa, loveseat & chair)*		
	Sweeping	***2*** *each (kitchen/ dining/ bathroom)*		
	Making Bed	***3*** *(only your own bed)*		
	Putting away clothes	***3*** *(clean clothes where they belong)*		
	Hoovering any room	***4*** *(one time a day)*		

	Sorting laundry	*4 (before it's washed)*		
	Folding clothes	*4 (after it's washed/dried)*		
	Wash dishes	*4 (cups/ silverware)*		
	Put away clean dishes	*4 (where they belong)*		
Other Stuff	Getting the mail	*2 (one time a day)*		
	Wearing seatbelt	*4 (anytime in a car)*		
	Not answering phone	*4 (anytime someone calls)*		
	Not answering door	*4 (anytime)*		

The way I figure it, the kids can earn 10 pennies a day just for the hygiene portion of this system. I will have to work out more privileges as time goes on. There will be immediate payment each day once something is done and the privileges can be purchased at certain times during the day and at the end of each week for the special ones like spending the night. I know that this will be time consuming for me to keep up with all the earnings, but I feel that this is a great investment. The plan is that the kids will help add up their pay. This will help them in their math skills. I have a container for each of the kids to keep their pennies in. We will be decorating the outside of the containers and personalizing them this afternoon. I do hope that they will like this new concept. I feel confident about it and I know that it will be a growing process for us all as I work out the kinks in it. Thank you, Father for giving me the opportunity to try this system. Thank you for the wisdom and confidence to implement it. May I continue to lean not on my understanding, but in all my ways acknowledge YOU! I know that I'm NOT in the darkness as the enemy will have me believe. **UPDATE NOTE:** *This has been working GREAT! I have found that if the kids want to watch a movie and they don't have enough pennies, they will run around and do more chores to collect the amount that they need. I have even witnessed LuLu sharing her earnings with Corey so that he can watch a movie with her. I do allow this—this is a great thing!! I've also started FREE Friday—which is a FREE movie night with the family! Games and other activities are FREE—I have done this twice a month for the last two months! The kids get excited when I put the homemade sign up on the refrigerator announcing it! A definite keeper!*

I could have filled this chapter with many more entries from my journal during these years that would cause a sincere sense of desperation and fear. I have chosen to omit most of those entries due to the fact that they leave me in such a dark place that I would rather not submit you to them. I will include more journal entries in the next chapters, but I will omit those entries that are too depressing or have little or no positive feelings. I am thankful for the times during these days in our wilderness journey when I was encouraged by the Father by the light of the moon. I was reminded of that famous line by a hotel chain stating that they "would leave the light on for you". Do you remember that slogan? I always thought that that was very hospitable of them. Spending the time in the middle of the night—alone—fearing to go to sleep in case *LuLu* decided to go outside and ride her bicycle, (true story—happened more than once! Thankful for caring neighbors!) I began to feel that the moon was my own private night light—lit by the Father to help me in the darkest times. My relationship with Him became stronger as I sat and talked with him each night—by the light of the moon.

"You are my lamp, O LORD;
the LORD turns my darkness into light."

2 Samuel 22:29

"You, O LORD, keep my lamp burning;
my God turns my darkness into light."

Psalm 18:28

Chapter 6

WONDERFUL WORKS OF WISDOM

With age comes wisdom. I could not wait for the years to pass to obtain the wisdom that I needed to be able to help my daughter—I needed wisdom THEN! I often prayed for wisdom beyond my years so that I could help my daughter through these rough times. I searched for books and advice but, if there were any books or resources that were available for me during the early years of my wilderness journey, I never found them. The internet was a new avenue that I was unfamiliar with and even if I did have access to it, I would not have known what to search for. I relied solely on the Father for all my problems with *LuLu*. I now believe that if I had found resources and support, I would not have had the opportunity to witness the miracles that I did. I would have missed them. I would have thought that the techniques that I was trying were working because of the resource and *not* miracles from the Father. It was very frustrating at the time, but now I see the significance. I try to remember that in other areas of my life—I may not understand what is going on, but I do trust that the Father will take care of me much better than I can take care of myself. That is a hard lesson to learn and I am thankful that I learned it early. I have to be honest and tell you that even though I learned it early, I still struggle from time to time—especially when I walk by *sight* and not by faith!

The following pages are taken from my partial journal entries. The content explains some of the wonderful wisdom that I received over the years during my journey in the wilderness from the Father to help me with the problems that I was experiencing. The wisdom that was documented in the previous chapter could have been included here, but I wanted to focus this chapter on just two categories: Problems and the solutions that worked.

I have chosen the journal entries during the time when *LuLu* was about ten years old. She had recently been tested in school and the results were disappointing. She was well below her age and grade level and because of this, she couldn't remain focused or engaged in class. She often acted out and disrupted the class out of sheer boredom. In working with her teacher and the school counselor, I prayed even more for wisdom for all of us so that she wouldn't be "lost" in the system. I knew that she could follow the simple rules of her classroom and we were determined to see that it carried over to our home life too. I began making a list of problems and solutions— what worked, what didn't. There were many failures and tears— both from me and *LuLu*. Failure is difficult—especially when you put all your energy and heart into it

September 2001

I have decided to add some additional things to my journal entries. I will document the problems and all the things that we did to solve them. I will follow up with the solutions that worked.

Problem: *We are struggling with LuLu talking back and arguing.*
Solution: *Things that did NOT work:*
- *Take things away*
- *Send her to her room*
- *Paddling*

Solution: *Things that DID work:*
- *Staying CALM*
- *Not arguing back*
- *Saying "Because you have CHOSEN to talk to me that way, you will not get to _____ (whatever she wanted to do) You need to apologize and try again." If protest ensures: "Would you like to miss 2 times of not _____? It's YOUR choice!" Saying this puts*

her in control over her actions and behavior and holds her accountable for her choices.

This has worked very well—so well that I'm using this with the boys too!

Problem: *LuLu has refused to listen to instruction by putting her hands over her ears and closing her eyes. This usually comes when I'm telling her something important about school or giving her correction and guidance.*

Solution: *I keep CALM and say "REWIND"—this lets her know that I'm giving her a chance to CHOOSE a better behavior and that my words will NOT be repeated. I have decided to say things to her only a few times—this way, she has to learn to listen. (Side Note: I still use this after all these years—yes, it still works!)*

This has worked so well that I'm also using it for the boys!

Problem: *LuLu has been getting into verbal and physical fights with her brothers. Some of them are very severe—more than just sibling rivalry.*

Solution: *When the fights are verbal, I say, "I'm about to call for peace. If you are talking after I call peace, then you lose two privileges and twenty pennies. If it continues, then you will receive twenty five licks with the paddle." I count slowly to three and if there is anyone who is still talking, I have to follow through with my plan. Remember, your words are only as good as the action that backs them up! Be prepared to do what you say you will do—be careful in choosing your words—you are the example!*

October 2001

Solution: that HAS worked with the fights are physical, I call for peace and let everyone know that our hands are for loving and not hurting one another.

Solution: that HAS brought great peace: <u>Family meetings</u>. During this time, the kids get to express their feelings. Everyone has a turn and to keep it fair we have a three minute time limit and I bought a rubber lemon for the person speaking to hold. It serves as a stress ball and a fun element. After all, everyone has a sour attitude once in a while—so why not? When you are holding the lemon, it's your turn to speak. We use feeling words: I feel . . . . hurt, upset, sad . . . . etc. When everyone has had a turn, I ask that each of them try to see the argument/ disagreement from the other person's point of view. I often ask them to pretend to be the other person and try to debate the opposite side's view. It has worked very well! (Although they didn't like it in the beginning because they only wanted to see their own side!) I have found that we have family meetings about once or twice a week and it tends to be very orderly. Keeper indeed! This will come in very handy as the kids get older!

Solution: that HAS worked with anger issues with LuLu: I took two empty plastic jars and painted the inside of them. I painted one RED (the color of anger) and the other one PINK (LuLu's favorite color at this time) We worked together to decorate each jar with stickers and drawings. The red jar is left empty but the pink jar is filled with slips of colored construction paper. Each slip of construction paper has a "happy thought" on it. LuLu and I sat at the table and thought about all the things that make her happy—example: "Spending girl time with mom". We must have at least 35 slips of paper in that jar! But that is okay! It's working!

The way it works: When LuLu gets angry, she gets out the "angry jar" and yells into it and replaces the lid. She then takes out as many slips of paper out of the "happy thoughts jar" and reads them until she is calm and feeling better. "Happy Thoughts" can always be added to the jar as time goes on and more happy experiences are realized. Once she has calmed down, the "angry jar" is taken outside and opened to let the anger go to the "angry place"(this is where she has said that the anger needs to go!)

Funny note: One day when we were outside letting the "anger" out of the jar, she made a comment just as a flock of birds was flying over us. "I sure hope that the "anger" doesn't hit those birds! If it does, they may poop on us!" SIDE NOTE: Have you ever wondered where the concept of "angry birds" came from? Well now you know! I should have submitted this idea years ago!

November 2001 LuLu turns 10 this month!

Problem: *Road trips—Road trips have been terrible!*

Solution: *The "to go bag"—this canvas bag (that I got at a yardsale for twenty five cents) contains all sorts of goodies—word searches, travel games, crayons and coloring books. The kids are not allowed to use these things while we are at home. LuLu is in charge of the "to go bag" and it's her job to get it ready before we get on the road. One particular game that the kids like is the I Spy game. However, LuLu gets very frusterated when she can't get the answers quickly and the fun time turns sour for everyone in the car. I think that I've solved* *this problem by making up short list for each of the kids (especially LuLu) to use individually. It looks something like this:*

I spy:

☐ *A boy wearing a hat*   ☐ *A blue truck*
☐ *Someone cutting grass*   ☐ *2 birds*
☐ *A swimming pool*   ☐ *A cow*
☐ *3 yellow lights*   ☐ *A house with a red door*
☐ *A barn*   ☐ *A basketball goal*
☐ *A library*

I made several cards like this—each one different— some are longer and some have pictures. LuLu seems to like this a whole lot and she looks forward to completing her card each time we get into the car. It's funny to hear her announce that she has spied another object on the list. This is so much better than hearing her scream and moan and complain.

Problem: Fear of the Vacuum Cleaner. For some reason, she has been scared of the vacuum cleaner for the longest time. I thought that she would grow out of it—she has not. Even at this age, she still runs and gets on the sofa or her bed and covers up with her sweet feet blankie.

Solution: I wanted to give LuLu a sense of peace during our cleaning times. I have decided to hot glue 2 large wiggly eyes on the front of the vacuum cleaner along with a large white pom pom nose. The vacuum cleaner is red and these accessories really make it stand out. I needed to come up with a name for our vacuum cleaner to make it more personable and since it's is a Hoover brand, I've decided to name it: "Hoover". I introduced "Hoover" today and LuLu smiled and was very calm while it was in front of her. A true miracle in itself! I explained that "Hoover" had a job like all of us. His job was to clean the floor of our house and "eat up" all the things that didn't belong on the floor. I went on to explain that the loud sound that he made was a warning to let people know that he was coming and to pick up anything off the floor that wasn't supposed to be there. (This will come in handy for getting her to pick up her room!) She seemed to like this explanation and started "talking" to "Hoover" and telling him about herself. She told him that she was sorry for being scared of him and that she will try her best to understand why he is so loud. I'm very proud of her! Thank you Father for this wonderful piece of wisdom! It's going to make our lives so much better!! ADDED NOTE: We just had a neighbor stop by and LuLu introduced the vacuum cleaner as "Hoover, our brother"! Too funny!

December 2001

We celebrated LuLu bday this month and she received a baby doll that looks almost real! It scared me as we put the batteries in it getting it ready to put down in the gift bag before we presented it to her. I hope that this baby doll will help with her nurturing skills and her feelings of empathy for others without causing any harm to any living thing. We have had to keep Mr. Socks, our cat away from her when we are not around due to the fact that she likes to put him in the dresser drawers or shut him up in various small spaces. Most of the spaces are too small for him. He is a Maine Coon cat and quite large. He is an indoor cat and declawed. I don't think that she is trying to injure him, just that she wants to see how many small places she can put him before he starts to meow. I'm hoping that this doll will help her get I in touch with her feelings for others.

Problem: <u>The doll has DIED!</u> *LuLu woke me up this morning in a sheer panic. The batteries in the doll that she received for her birthday last month are weak and are apparent in the doll's speech and actions. LuLu FREAKED OUT and was begging me to help her "baby". She stated that she loved the baby and she didn't want it to die! I reassured her that it was just the batteries running down and that we would replace them and then the baby would be fine. I searched all over the house and found no replacement batteries.*

LuLu continued to beg me to help her baby—to save her—she was very hysterical—hyperventilating—the boys woke up and began laughing at her because she thought that the baby doll was really alive. I was so angry at them for teasing her and angry at myself for thinking that she should have known the difference in a doll and a live person. I sat with her on the floor of her bedroom, tears streaming down her face—her arms wrapped tightly around her baby doll and rocking as if trying to console it—just as a parent would do. I sent the boys out of the room as I got down on the floor with her and tried to explain that this baby doll was NOT a real, live person—even though she had similar actions. She didn't seem to understand, she only continued to cry and beg me to help her baby doll. She grabbed my clothes as she cried and begged—it broke my heart. Robby ended up going and getting some batteries for the baby doll. I was hoping to teach her compassion and love with this baby doll, but I think that I may have underestimated the reaction and attachment that she has to it. I know that she has a difficult time separating fantasy from reality. I will do better in the future to make sure that she realizes what it living and what is just a toy or doll. We all learned for this experience.

Solution: Have a backup set of batteries specifically for the baby doll—and use this as a learning tool about great responsibility choices. (realizing the time when the batteries need to be changed and learning how to change the batteries herself and ask for help instead of getting angry)

January 2002

Problem: <u>*Hearing voices of hate.*</u> *LuLu has been telling me that she is hearing someone talk to her. She says that she is being told that she is stupid and doesn't deserve to live! She says that she hears this voice all the time and sometimes it sounds like ME! I reassured her that I would NEVER say anything hurtful like that to her! She hugged me and then she began to cry! She stated that she is very scared and that she wishes that the voices would just shut up and go away! Oh Father, what is going on? What do I do? Please help me!*

Solution: *A lot of prayer and reassurance! I have also decided to play Christian music in her room all the time. Sometimes it's little kid music, other times it's radio music on a Christian radio station. I have also put the Bible on tape in her room to play after she is asleep. I'm doing my best to fill her with the Word of God. I will NOT give up OR give in!*

February 2002

Problem: <u>*Telling about things differently than they actually happened.*</u> *It seems that LuLu can remember things that happened over two years ago, but can't recall the events of the school day. If she happens to remember, it's nothing like what actually happened. She often tells* *it like SHE sees it—which is often misunderstood and slightly on the fantasy side.*

*   **Solution**: *Reminding her to talk about her day's events and we talk about if they really happened that way or not. We take the time to think about her day from the time that she got up in the morning all the way through until bedtime. I often throw in a crazy event like: "after breakfast, LuLu rode an elephant to school"(instead of the bus)—we laugh and she corrects it. We often play the "Do we" game. It's just a game that I made up to help her learn the difference between fantasy—the things that she sees on t.v. and in books, and real life. It goes like this. I usually begin the game at the times that she is looking restless or bored and begin by asking: "Do we ride to school on elephants?" Then she would answer, "No, we don't ride to school on elephants. We ride to school in a school bus." This game has been applied to all areas of our lives—like the food that we eat and the way young ladies are expected to behave. I remember one day asking the question: "Do we wear our socks on our hands?" her reply was, "Yes, we wear socks on our hands when we have lost our gloves." (Now I understand why she was wearing her shoes without her socks one day!)*

*   **Problem**: <u>Disagreeing on clothes to wear to school.</u> *Even though we would pick out something the night before, "LuLu" would have a problem with it the next morning and the whole day would start off terrible.*

*   **Solution:** *Sunday afternoons are spent getting clothes ready for the school week. I know that there are some days that I just don't feel like wearing what I picked out the night before, and I'm sure that LuLu may feel the same way. So, I picked up a hanging closet bag from a yard sale that has five compartments in it with the labels*

Monday-Friday on it. We both agree on five sets of clothes—shirts, pants, socks and hair bows. It's her job to place them in each compartment. We have agreed that she can wear Monday's clothes on Wednesday if she wants to, but that she can only choose the clothes that are in the compartments—no Halloween costumes or pajamas are allowed.

This has helped tremendously!! I can't begin to explain how much easier this is—especially since I gave her limited choices—she feels in control and is able to make some choices for herself—a great learning tool!

* * * * * *

While many of these solutions happened over a long period of time, there was still a lot of wisdom to come. We continued to struggle in many areas but, our darkness was getting a little lighter and we could see how far we'd truly come thanks to the journal entries that I'd been keeping. Even though it was very difficult to take the time to write down all the detailed information, I know that it was well worth it in the long run!

"But the wisdom that comes from heaven is first of all pure; then peace-loving, considerate, submissive, full of mercy and good fruit, impartial and sincere."

James 3:17

Chapter 7

MIRACLES IN THE MIDST OF MADNESS

It seems like I've always heard the old saying that it's always darkest before the dawn and not truly understood it until I went through this wilderness journey. When things seemed hopeless and I was growing weary in my daily walk, I was often pleasantly surprised with unexpected miracles. It was like little gifts from the Father! When I was a little girl, I would always ask for a "prize" (surprise) from the store when I was unable to go. I usually got M&Ms as they are my favorite, but occasionally I received something unexpected—something greater than the smaller thing that I asked for. The Father works like this too! He answers our prayers with more than what we ask for. I witnessed His benevolence many times during our journey with *LuLu*. I will try as best as I can to relay some of the miracles that I witnessed first-hand. The miracles came not by the fact that I deserved them, because often I did not, but by the grace and love of the Father. Often I didn't deserve the M&Ms either, but this is how the Father works. He is a loving parent, full of grace and compassion. He knows the desires of our hearts and gives us what we really need too!

The following journal pages are mixed with both days of madness and days of miracles. I hope that you will be able to see the Father's light shining through it all.

I am reminded of the many diagnoses that we got in *LuLu* early life. The future outlook was not good. We were given advice from all sides—much of it negative. I have to tell you that when you feel like you're surrounded, and all your tears are gone, the Father will send you a miracle that you didn't see coming. Communication is the key—you can't let it all be one sided. Faith is also part of it—

even if it's as small as a mustard seed. Sometimes I felt that my faith was just that small. I was faithful to pray and talk to God, but I wasn't seeing many changes in *LuLu's* behavior or condition. I guess I expected an immediate miracle like those healings in the Bible. The miracles *did* come, however, they were not immediate. I now know why I was allowed to experience these miracles slowly. I don't think that I could have appreciated the grandness and the true change if it had come about suddenly. I wouldn't be writing this book now and God wouldn't be glorified by this story.

The following journal pages are a condensed version from when we were going through some intense times and span several years and range from the accounts of doctor visits to *LuLu's* high school graduation. It is my hope that you will be encouraged as you read about each of her triumphs. I have *not* included some parts of the journal entries at "LuLu's" request. They are not important parts of the whole story and I have to honor her wishes.

March 2003

Today we will be going to see a new doctor. Her name is Renee Winters with Mental Health. I do hope that is not another run around like we've experienced in the past. I've tried for years to get LuLu some help! Oh, please, please, please, let this be the thing that gets her help! We've either been financially unable to obtain the right help, her behavior has been too explosive, or we don't qualify for some reason. I pray that this puts us in contact with just the right people.

Well, I don't know what to say. I'm at a loss for words. I feel that Mrs. Winters doesn't believe anything that I told her about LuLu and her behavior and actions. She was a perfect "angel" while we were in her office and even SMILED! I was trying to tell Mrs. Winters things and then she would turn and ask LuLu if I was telling the truth—

of course LuLu smiled and said that I was not! Father, please help me! I thought that surely this would be our avenue of greater assistance! Please show me the way!! I will take LuLu to see Mrs. Winters every week for the rest of the month and hopefully see some improvement and receive some help.

April 2003

Well, I must admit that I was hoping for better results from Mrs. Winters. I will not be taking LuLu back to see her. Today was the very last straw! When I offered to show her my journal pages, she pointed her finger at me and said that I could have just written random stuff down to make LuLu look bad! What? I can't believe it! I've still been dealing with terrible mornings and nights—she doesn't want to go to bed at night and she doesn't want to get up in the mornings! I am at loss. I am feeling more and more helpless! I have made several calls to local doctors and I'm hoping that I can get her in to see one of them with in the month!

April 2003

Father, I feel like I'm in a tornado that is never ending! It's constantly spinning—I'm always confused and feeling so alone in this battle. I know that you are with me, but I can't seem to find you! I'm so scared and I'm all out of tears. I want my mom so badly! I feel like I'm not a very good mother! I've tried everything I know to do to help my little girl and she can't get past the tantrums—she is almost thirteen! Lord, please help me!

April 2003

We finally saw a new doctor today! His name is Dr. Maxwell and he gave LuLu some meds that will help her to stop hearing the voices and other sounds. I hope that he is right about that! He seemed a bit stuffy—although he was nice. We will go back to see him next month.

May 2003

These past few months have been very difficult. There have been too many tantrums to count. We never know what will set her off and we are all walking around on egg shells. This month, while the boys were outside waiting for the bus, LuLu was inside screaming and pitching a fit because and because she wanted to be first in line to get on the bus and because she wasn't first in line, she didn't want to go to school. I told her that if she wanted to be the first in line for the bus, then she should have gotten outside first—before the boys did. I also told her that she can't always be first—that we have to take turns and share . . . . she didn't like that advice one bit! She continued to scream everyday—for various reasons—it seemed like each day was worse. I walked out one day just before the boys got on the bus. LuLu was still inside screaming and kicking holes in the wall. A neighbor was walking her dog and happened to pass by our house and heard her screams. The neighbor asked the boys if they lived in the house—they both shook their heads—denying that they were even remotely a part of such a wild family.

It seems that nothing that we do helps my daughter. The severe mood swings, the yelling, growling, stealing, destroying things, hurting herself and others—I'm at a total loss as what else to do! We've seen doctors, we've stood our ground, we have cried out of anger, despair and sheer exhaustion and we see little change in her behavior. Lord, I don't know what else to do! I have not lost my faith in YOU! I know that you are still working in her life! Please show me a miracle! Please!!

June 2003-July 2003

Summer is in full swing around our house and LuLu has not stopped complaining from the time that she gets up every day until she goes to bed at night. She is angry that the sun is shining because it's too bright—she's angry that the moon is out and that it's dark outside—she is angry that there are t.v. commercials interrupting her favorite show—she is angry that it's raining—she stays angry—all the time. We never see her smile and she often causes some kind of physical harm to herself or to her brothers at the slightest upset. I don't know what else to do! I feel like I'm going to burst! I'm so miserable! I feel that I have no one else that understand this—It's been a great help writing all this down, but I wonder what I will gain from it, other than feelings of depression should I ever have to read it again! I want the medical staff to stop telling me to change my parenting techniques—they truly have NO idea what kind of parent I am! They don't know how many hours that I've put in with her—the long, drawn out hours that I've spent teaching her new ways to learn things— the countless hours spent awake, making sure that as she plays in her room at 2am that she doesn't leave the house in the middle of the night—hours spent together—no one know how many hours I pray—on my knees before the Father—it seems like no one cares—maybe they don't— but I love my daughter and I will do everything I can for her—I will NOT give up!

We've seen Mrs. Winters again this month and I don't think that it's helping too much. I tried to talk to her about several things that we were having a problem with and she told me that she needed to talk to LuLu alone and that I could find a seat in the next room. The look on LuLu's face was that of sheer disgust for me as I left. I don't know what LuLu shared with her—probably MORE LIES—I wonder if these visits are just a waste of time!

July 2003-August 2003

I cannot begin to count all the holes in LuLu's room! She has kicked so many holes in her walls that it makes me want to cry! Robby and I worked so very hard on her room to make it a beautiful calming retreat for her! From the soft pink paint on the walls to the wide ballerina border at the top . . . . now it looks like it's a war zone!

She has continued to tell us all that she hates us. She degrades herself and the rest of us! She continues to squeeze Mr. Socks and shove him into small spaces. She is getting bigger and harder for me to handle. She is growing in strength too. I have a difficult time trying to make sure that she doesn't hurt herself or the boys. I don't know what to do!

This afternoon, as we were getting ready for baths and supper time, LuLu protested more than usual. She shoved me and caused me to fall. She ran to her room and began to break things. I am tired of no one believing that she acts like this, so I thought that I would video tape her. I got the camera out and began to record. As I got to her room, she saw me and growled and charged toward the camera— hitting it and hitting my right cheek bone under my right eye with the camera. I ran out of the room thinking that my eye was busted. It wasn't—it was just severely bruised! I feel so scared!! I want so badly to find the help for her—I just don't know what to do!! I feel like a prisoner in my own house! All I wanted was a little princess—to love and cherish! I feel like I'm being punished! Oh Lord, why do I feel this way!? I love you and I know that you haven't left me! What am I doing wrong!? Why can't I see any improvement? Please, Lord, hear my pleas for help!! I know that you can make all things work for good for those who love you! Please Father!

LuLu's new "thing" is that she feels that her face and hand are "sticky". She washes them constantly and has made them both very raw. Any medicine that I put on it causes her skin to sting—thus causing her to spin into an unending world-wind of chaos.

Today was my final breaking point! LuLu came at me and attacked me today! I was so scared! I called the doctor for him only to tell me that I needed to take her to the emergency room. He told me to call ahead and let them know that we were coming. I called Robby and he came straight home from work—but by the time he arrived, she had calmed down and was coloring in her room. I felt like we should continue on with the plan and take her to the E.R.—Robby agreed.

We waited in the E.R. for over two hours and it cost us $150! We were referred to the children's mental ward in Opelika. LuLu's only concern is about the windowless room that she heard the referring doctor tell us about. She says that she will need to know if it's day or night and she was NOT happy about the thought of being in a room without a window. As I write this, it's 1am and I'm wondering if we did the right thing by taking her to Opelika. Everyone is very upset in this house right now. The boys were still shaken by what they witnessed earlier with her attacking me and Robby is crying on the bed beside me as I write. I will try and get some rest tonight—

although I know that she is probably very scared right now—she is with strangers and I wonder if she feels that we have abandoned her—given up on her—Father, please bring her comfort and peace tonight—cover us all with your love.

9:15am

I've been up for a while. I just called to check on LuLu. I can not ask for her by name. I have to use a confidential patient number code. I was told by the nurse that answered that she was an excellent patient and that they had had no problems with her obeying them. I couldn't believe my ears! I asked if she was SURE that we were talking about the same person. She assured me that we were—I don't believe it! I didn't want her to act badly for them, but at the same time, I want people to believe me when I tell them about her behavior. She is probably acting like a little angel because they have not told her "No" yet. I suggested that the staff do that and the nurse stated that they would try it. Although she was a bit cautious of wanting to keep her another night we agreed that she would indeed stay. She told me that I could come and get her if I wanted to. I was told that all kids go through a "honeymoon period" and that her true self should emerge tomorrow and that they would be willing to keep her for one more night.

8:30pm

We all spoke to LuLu tonight before she went to bed. She sounded so sweet! I sure wish that she would be like that for us! We will be traveling tomorrow afternoon to pick her up!

The next day: Well, we went and picked LuLu up this afternoon. As we were talking with the doctors, she sat very still and quiet and our hopes were high that she had indeed changed. The doctors told us that they had had no problems with her whatsoever and that we should continue to seek counseling for all of us. They went on to say that they didn't see our reasons for even wanting to admit her into the hospital and that we should consider how our home life affects her. I wanted to scream! I wanted to just cry and tell them about all the years of struggles that we have been through. I didn't. Something held my tongue tight in my mouth and all I could manage was a smile. A SMILE! Just the OPPOSITE of what I wanted to do! They went on to tell us that they didn't see a bright future for her. They admitted that they saw some severe delays and that she would most likely not be able to complete school, or even obtain and retain a job. I couldn't see how they could even know that at this time. I refuse to believe that—I don't accept it! I know that the Father has a plan for her—a special plan—and I will NOT accept the report that we got from the doctors! It's just like the ones from all the other doctors! We didn't like what they said, but we listened quietly out of respect. We left with our feelings hurt and our wallet a lot thinner, but no further than when we arrived!

As we got into the car, all our hopes came to a halt! She began to kick the back of my seat and hit her head on the door window. We don't know what set her off. We stopped at the gas station and offered to get her a Sprite— she screamed that she didn't want one and continued to scream, growl and kick the back of my seat. When Robby got back in the car without her Sprite, she became more violent! We reminded her that she had said that she didn't want one. We stood firm and didn't go back and get her one. She continued to scream all the way back home—

some 70 miles! She kept repeating that she wished that she had just stayed at the hospital and NEVER come home! I'm sure that we will continue to hear this many times in the days to come!

September 2003-December 2003

During these past few months, I feel like we have wasted our time seeing Mrs. Winters. I'm often told to wait out in the other room as she talks and plays with LuLu. I am bothered by this because LuLu continues to tell lies and she continues to ramble about things that either happened on t.v., in the past or that she made up. She seems to combine the many stories into one—both fantasy and reality and often the person listening has to be aware that this is what is happening. Mrs. Winter has no clue because she refused to let me tell her. I tried several different times to tell her and each time she told me that she would make her own assessment. She seems more agitated after each session with Mrs. Winters and I don't look forward to taking her each week. I plan on asking for a transfer . . . . I'm sure that that will not go over well, but I have to do what is best for my daughter.

Our last session with Mrs. Winters last week didn't go very well. LuLu began to ramble about things that were off subject and I was called in to explain. I told Mrs. Winters bluntly that I had tried unsuccessfully in the past to tell her about these ramblings and that I was quickly excused to the other room. I sat quietly and smiled as she continued to ramble on about things that made no sense—no point—no common thread—a lot of jumping from fantasy to reality and back again. As I left today, I asked that we be sent to another counselor. Mrs. Winters looked both shocked and relieved. I couldn't tell which—I know that I'm relieved!

Well, it's almost the end of 2003! I feel that I have been in an unending race this year! I am totally exhausted and I hope that next year will bring about positive changes for LuLu and all of us! Please Father, may you hear our cry and move mightily!

The next two years were very much of the same. We saw little improvement in *LuLu's* behavior at home. Her behavior at school struggled as she moved through each grade level, falling further and further behind—both socially and mentally. She continued to have little or no friends. No one came to spend the night, attend a birthday party or even invite her to one. She had some good days and for those we were very thankful! Often there would be many days of struggle and conflict and only a half day of peace. We learned to cherish those half days and be thankful for the miracles that they brought. We refused to give up on her! We worked with her on hygiene, manners and speech. Some days were easy and others were very trying. Some days would seem like we were starting all over again from the toddler stage. Constant prayer and journaling kept me sane. I don't even like to read all the entries of the journal during that time—that is why it has been omitted here. I could only find pages and pages of despair and depression and I didn't want to share any more of that with you! I wanted to focus on the miracles . . . .

The year 2006 brought us the first large wave of miracles that we were seeking! It seemed like wherever we turned we saw another miracle! We had experienced miracles in the past but nothing could prepare us for the elation that we felt as we witnessed one miracle after another! I can't begin to tell you how excited we were to experience them. Many people who were in our lives as the miracles took place credited the changes to the things that Robby and I had done. We were quick to let them know that it was *not* us—that it was <u>all</u> God!

There were a lot of positive changes in our lives during 2006! *LuLu's* behavior at school had improved quite a bit as I had to go toe to toe with her Jr. High school counselors to get her moved up to the special education contained class up at the high school. I was a long term substitute at the high school and since her school got out 30 minutes earlier than the high school, she would ride the bus up the hill and spend the remainder of the school day in the special ed. Contained class. The teacher of the contained class welcomed her with open arms and refused to let her just sit and visit with the other students. She gave her work just like the other students and it helped her so very much! She was not learning the life skills that she needed at her present school and I knew that she would need to know the simple things like her address and phone number.—At the end of the school year I went to the County board of education and was given the go ahead to enroll her into the high school program. I was so happy!

The battle was difficult and I had the very people that I had depended on to help me with *LuLu* turn on me! Her school counselors argued that she would be lost in the contained class. That she would be higher functioning than most of her peers in that class. While I did see their point, I had to do what I could to ensure that she would not "fall through the cracks" and be truly lost in the school system. I felt that I was doing what was best for her—and looking back, I was right! She just blossomed in the contained class! The move to the contained class was just what she needed! She became a happier person and her outbursts became rare. She had friends for the first time and she was truly happy with herself. I'm so glad that I made the choice to move her. Even if it was against all that the "professionals" thought was the best for her, I heard the voice of the Lord strong and clear.

The following is a journal entry from the end of 2006. *LuLu* was in her first year in the contained special education class at the high school. She had become a different person during this year. No one knew of the battles and struggles that we had faced and fought all those years ago. For me, they seemed like an eternity ago—but in reality; they were only just a few years in the past. I knew that one day I would write a book documenting the miracles of God in the life of our precious daughter and I'm thankful for the journals that I kept during my time in the "wilderness".

December 2006

This year has brought so many changes! So many positive changes. We continue to see Dr. Brown and Dr. Smitherman and the changes in LuLu are so great! If I could sum it up in one word, it would have to be "miracle" without a doubt! This year has given LuLu the opportunity to learn to talk about her feelings and not act upon them. We have also worked very closely with her teachers and bus driver to give her more stability and structure between our house and the school environment. She has learned that taking a bath can be fun if you add bubbles and Barbies! Our meal times are more pleasant as we take turns telling different parts of the same fairytale story. Bedtime has become a fun time for us as we read books together 30 minutes before lights out. Our trips have gotten better with the "to go bag" and I can't begin to explain the peace that covers our house! I'm so thankful for all the miracles in the midst of the madness. I do not know at this time what the purpose was for our "wilderness journey" but I can tell you that I know that I'm stronger for having experienced it.

May 2010

Well, she did it! Our LuLu has graduated high school! I am so very proud of her that I can't contain myself! I never believed the doctors when they told me that she was not going to be a productive ciziten or that she would never have any sort of normal life! They were soooo wrong! My face hurts from smiling and my tears of joy are overflowing! LuLu walked across that stage tonight with confidence and determination! She looked so beautiful in her lime green and black dress as we walked out the door tonight to attend her graduation. Her smile said it all! She was happy and proud of herself—as she should be! I know that her future will be anything but easy, but I'm ready! I'm not about to give up now! Praise you Father for blessing me with my beautiful daughter and for preparing me for the journey.

Chapter 8

THERE'S A KNOT IN MY BED!

As I consider some of the special times that *LuLu* and I have shared over the years, I think about the bed time routine that she invented one summer night. It happened as we were about to read our nightly bedtime stories. I was in the kitchen just finishing up washing the dishes from supper. *LuLu* yelled for me to come, to come *quick*! I thought something was wrong so I ran from the kitchen straight to her bedroom—the yellow, rubber gloves still on my hands—dripping water everywhere! I must have been a sight to see because she laughed and giggled for the longest time. When I asked her what the matter was, she pointed down to the end of her bed where her feet were wiggling under the covers. She giggled and said that there were "knots" in her bed! We both laughed and I tried (unsuccessfully) to "catch" the "knots". She moved her little legs so fast that I couldn't keep up with them! This routine became one that would last many years and even now, at age twenty-one, she still enjoys having "knots" in her bed from time to time.

I wrote a little poem in my journal about the "knots" in *LuLu's* bed.

Hurry, Mom! Hurry and come as quick as a blink!
Just leave those dishes there in the sink!

"There's a knot in my bed!" LuLu said!
It's here and it's there! It's everywhere!

Mom's yellow, rubber gloves, still wet from the sink
Can't catch the knots—they're as quick as a wink!

We laugh and we giggle
As her little feet wiggle

Every night they will appear,
I don't know why they're here,
Other than to bring us much needed laughter and cheer!

In my heart, these times will remain,
Bedtime will never be truly the same!

Chapter 9

CHOICES

Our lives are full of choices. Just consider the choices that you made today. You chose to get up on time or sleep late, what to wear, what to eat for breakfast (or you chose not to eat breakfast at all) and you chose what kind of attitude you were going to have. You probably chose a specific route to work or if you work from home, you may have chosen several goals to accomplish today. Needless to say that our choices each day are unlimited and it's how we chose that determines our future. If I chose to wear the cute shoes that rub my heal, I would be very miserable by the end of the day. Sometimes we don't consider the consequences of our choices (even if the shoes are that cute!) until we have had to "walk all day in those uncomfortable shoes." Being parents puts an extra responsibility on our choices. The choices that we make at any given time will affect our children now and in the future. If we want to leave them a legacy, an honorable heritage, then we must carefully consider our choices.

As a long-term substitute at the local high school, I would always tell the students to make their time count for positive things. I would tell them that we are each given 86,400 seconds each day and that our lives can change in any one of those seconds. I went on to tell them that their tomorrows are determined by the choices that they make today. I encouraged them to always make good choices even if it was difficult. Even if they were the only ones standing up for what was right, it would be well worth it in the future. I loved my job as a substitute and from what I'm told; I was pretty good at it. I learned a lot about myself and how God was using my wilderness experience to benefit others. I learned to help encourage those that were struggling with poor choices and help them make a difference in their tomorrows. I now understand that my experience in the wilderness was far more reaching than I could have even imagined. I was a permanent fixture at the high school for six years and in that time, God used me to positively affect hundreds of lives. It's not uncommon for me to run across former students (many of them have started families of their own) and have them tell me that they are using their 86,400 seconds for positive things! Those words are music to my ears—not only because they are doing positive things with their time, but because I chose to be a willing vessel for the Lord and He chose me to carry out His plan.

I have to honestly say that I have no regrets about the choices that I made during my journey in the wilderness. I may have wished that some choices were made earlier and some were made later, but I think that I would still make the same choices today. We learn by our mistakes and I learned a lot through my journey with *LuLu*. I know that many of my friends and family thought (and maybe still think) that we were (are) too hard on her and the boys. To those people, I say this:

I feel that I have prepared my children for life without me. I have given them the tools that they will need to live independently. I have taught them to think for themselves and expect consequences for their poor choices. I have loved them enough to allow them to learn from their mistakes without stepping in to help them. I have cried in the silence of the night because I have refused to step in and save them from a learning experience even though I know that their choices will bring them pain and heartache and I have learned to not let go too soon or hold on to long.

It's funny that one of my pet peeves is unruly and undisciplined children, especially since we had such a time with *LuLu*. But my thoughts are that if we have high standards for our children, even those with delays, then we are forming a better world for us all. This life is cruel and full of things that are unfair. I feel that if we can prepare our children to think for themselves and be that change that we want to see, then we all win. I don't claim to be an expert on parenting, I only speak from my experience. I feel that if we are consistent and stand firm on our word, then we cannot lose. We, as adults, are expected to follow the rules (laws) of this land—like stopping at a red light. If we choose not to, we have to suffer the consequences of a traffic ticket, or worse, death. I want my children to be that positive change in the world and I believe that we can create a better tomorrow for our children by preparing them today.

I'm thankful that God chose me to travel this journey. I know that He has chosen more paths for me and that many journeys lay ahead. I am comforted to know that I will not be alone and that I will be better at the end of the journey than I was at the beginning.

As we continue to travel on in our journeys of this life, I know that there will be many paths that are narrow and less traveled. It is my hope that I will continue to choose those paths and keep my focus on The Father. I hope for you, dear reader, that my story has given you some encouragement and some hope in your journey and to ensure you that you are not alone! Our days may not be perfect or go the way that we would have planned, but we can always choose to see the good and the positive if we just look for it!

"You did not choose me, but I chose you and appointed you so that you might go and bear fruit—fruit that will last—and so that whatever you ask in my name the Father will give you."

John 15:16

". . . choose for yourselves this day whom you will serve, . . . as for me and my household, we will serve the LORD."

Joshua 24:15

Chapter 10

A SPECIAL NOTE FROM *LuLu*

I have heard that it takes a special kind of person to take care of a special needs child. Some parents of special needs children may not consider themselves blessed, but all children are a gift from God and He must have thought a lot of them to give them such a special gift. I'm so grateful that I didn't give up on her and that I was able to depend on the heavenly Father. I am so proud of the young woman that she has become! She has overcome more obstacles than I can count and beaten the odds that were stacked up against her. She has become a very productive citizen despite the reports from the doctors that she would not. I rejoice in the fact that I was part of the miracles that God performed in her life. I know that her purpose is even more than I could possibly understand, even now, but I'm thankful that the Father chose me to be her mother!

Thank you dear reader for allowing me to share a little part of my "wilderness journey" with you. Thank you for allowing me to share with you my life with a dandelion—my precious "blow-it flower!.

A special note from *LuLu* just For the Parents of special needs children: *There are some things I'd like you to remember as a parent of a special needs child. Please be patient. Even though it seems impossible to reach your child, don't stop trying! It may seem very difficult for you to understand what your child is going through. They may not be able to tell you but please let them be as independent as they can be. There may be something that they may not get to do, or may not understand but don't let their limitations limit them. Encourage them to try new things even if they fail.*

Giving them the chance to try will mean more to them than you know. It's like a staircase; you start at the bottom and work your way to the top—taking one step at a time. There may be things or a skill that they are good at. For example, they may be a blessing to other people by just listening to what they have to say . . . just by listening to all different people's stories about their lives. It really means a lot to people if you just take the time to listen to them. Everyone wants to feel important and loved. Encourage your child and love them for who God created them to be. He has an important job for them to do so please let them do it and don't hold them back. Our lives are like an unfinished painting—painted by the Master painter Himself. The whole picture of our lives can't be seen until we draw our last breath and then our family and friends see the true purpose of our lives. We need to make sure that our life is one that will be remembered for the glory and honor that we brought to God and how we shared His love with others while our life's painting was being finished.

A special note just for my special needs friends: *I say this to you— please don't give up! Life may be dark like a cave and there will be obstacles in your life that you don't understand but don't give up . . . things WILL get better as you learn to hear the voice of God. Please know that people WILL look at you differently and treat you differently because of your limitations. People WILL judge you before they get to know you. Don't let that stop you from being who you are.*

Make goals for yourself and think about all the things you CAN do and don't worry about the things you can't do. Be yourself! You were created for a greater purpose than you may realize, so be happy with who you are! No one has a perfect life . . . we just need to have thankful heart for the things that we're blessed with. Even though it seems hard and it may be a challenge, be strong and courageous. If life was easy and we had no challenges, then we wouldn't grow stronger, and become the person we were meant to be. I have faith